The world of networking brought to life before your eyes!

Expand your knowledge on additional topics with these full-color guides from Que!

Computers Illustrated shows you in full color:

- What happens when you turn on your PC

- How your machine loads and runs programs

- Where the information goes that you type in

- How monitors, printers, and modems work

- What goes on within the operating system

Programming Illustrated shows you in full color:

- What happens when a computer program runs

- How a programmer writes a Windows application

- Why a program works like it does

- How DOS, Windows, OS/2, and Mac programming differ

- What loops, clauses, and instructions are

Upgrading Your PC Illustrated shows you in full color:

- How to upgrade a computer's processor and memory

- What's needed to install a disk drive, modem, or sound card

- How to add a mouse, printer, game port, or video system

Networking
Illustrated

Eddie Kee

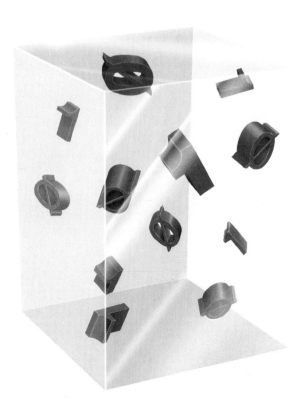

System
Scheduler

NIC
Device
Driver

Operating
System
Kernel

Physical
LAN

Server
Application
Programs

que

Networking Illustrated

Library of Congress Catalog No.: 94-67595

ISBN: 1-56529-893-4

97 96 95 94   4 3 2 1

Interpretation of the printing code: the rightmost double-digit number is the year of the book's printing; the rightmost single-digit number, the number of the book's printing. For example, a printing code of 94-1 shows that the first printing of the book occurred in 1994.

Publisher: David P. Ewing

Associate Publisher: Michael Miller

Publishing Director: Brad R. Koch

Managing Editor: Michael Cunningham

Marketing Manager: Greg Wiegand

Credits

Publishing Manager
C. Kazim Haidri

Acquisitions Editor
Angela J. Lee

Production Editor
Thomas F. Hayes

Copy Editor
Lori L. Cates

Technical Editors
Dennis A. Teague
Discovery Computing, Inc.

Acquisitions Coordinator
Patricia J. Brooks

Book Designer
Amy Peppler-Adams

Cover Designer
Dan Armstrong
Amy Peppler-Adams

Production Team
Jeff Baker
Angela D. Bannan
Anne Dickerson
Claudia Bell
Karen Dodson
Joelynn Gifford
Michael Hughes
Debbie Kincaid
Tim Montgomery
Nanci Sears Perry
Wendy Ott
Dennis Sheehan
Sue VandeWalle
Mary Beth Wakefield

Composed in *New Baskerville* by Que Corporation.

About the Author

Eddie Kee is a computer and networking consultant in northeastern Ohio. He has written chapters on networking in other Que books, including *Using Netware 3.12*, SE and *Using UNIX*, SE. As a consultant he specializes in installing, managing, and customizing networks for various applications. He is a member of IEEE, ACM, and Novell's professional developers program. He can be reached through CompuServe at 73165,526.

Dedication

To my very special and loving wife, Diane.

Acknowledgments

Like a Phoenix rising out of the ashes, so has *Networking Illustrated*. At the beginning of this book we had a fire at home that disrupted the entire working process. Through the patience of all the people at Que and many extra late nights, this book was completed.

The writing of a book of this nature requires the help and support of many people. Chris Haidri and Tom Hayes of Que and I spent many hours faxing illustrations and text back and forth, and lots and lots and lots of telephone time. The culmination of these efforts is found thoughout these pages. I also would like to thank those who have spent so many hours in colorizing the illustrations, organizing the information, and ultimately publishing this book.

No acknowledgment could be complete without recognizing my parents, Shirley and Don, and two very special grandmothers who celebrated their 90th birthdays this year. Happy birthday grandmas and thank you to all!!!

Trademark Acknowledgments

All terms mentioned in this book that are known to be trademarks or service marks have been appropriately capitalized. Que cannot attest to the accuracy of this information. Use of a term in this book should not be regarded as affecting the validity of any trademark or service mark.

Networking Illustrated

Table of Contents

What is a Network?

Basic Network Concepts

The OSI Model

Network Topologies

Cabling and Connections

Communication
Protocols

Operating Systems

Network-to-Network
Connections

MANs and WANs

Protecting
Network Data

Introduction

Hello. I'm glad you could join us for an illustrated tour of computer networks. *Networking Illustrated* was designed and developed to show you how the pieces of a computer network fit together, and what is really happening deep inside a network. This book covers topics ranging from application sharing to wireless communications. We introduce you to the latest networking buzzwords and the hardware and software associated with these buzzwords. We also try to show you, in visual form, how the hardware and software items on a network interrelate.

Computer networks are becoming increasingly common. There are very few offices that don't have at least one network interconnecting personal computers and printers. As the information super-highway becomes reality, more and more aspects of life outside of the workplace will involve sophisticated communications which were unimaginable until quite recently. Understanding network components can help you to understand the myriad technologies that soon will dominate the way you live individually and the way you interact with the rest of society.

Each two-page spread has one main illustration or several smaller illustrations. These illustrations provide the theme for the entire discussion on that topic, and allow you to visualize the concepts being discussed.

This column is the Background column. It provides general information about the topic presented in the illustration(s) on each two-page spread.

Chapter 6—Communication Protocols

The source stations all wait with information to be sent until a go signal is received. Once the go signal, or token, is received, that packet—and only that packet—of information is sent.

A token is much like a train signal. It signals the sending station to allow a train to leave a station, in much the same way a token is sent to a node to allow the node to release its packet of information. Only one packet can be on the network at a time, just as only one train at a time is allowed out of a station.

Token-Based Networks

Token-passing networks such as ARCnet and IBM Token Ring incorporate a signaling mechanism. This mechanism is used to control which stations on a network can send information and when they can do so. As in a train yard, only the node with the token (the "go" signal) can send information. The information is then allowed to travel to its destination. Once it arrives at the destination, an acknowledgment can be sent to the starting station.

100

We all come in contact with a common network daily—the telephone network. This network carries our conversations across the street or as far as to the other side of the world. Computer networks are merely an extension of the same technologies, a conglomeration of complicated equipment that becomes less complicated when you look at it piece-by-piece. To understand a whole computer network requires a basic understanding of its parts, and that's what this book helps you to do.

Hold on as we begin our networking journey.

These paragraphs of text move you smoothly through each illustration, pointing out and explaining certain items that deserve extra attention. Also included occasionally throughout the book are technical tips to help when you work with the item under discussion.

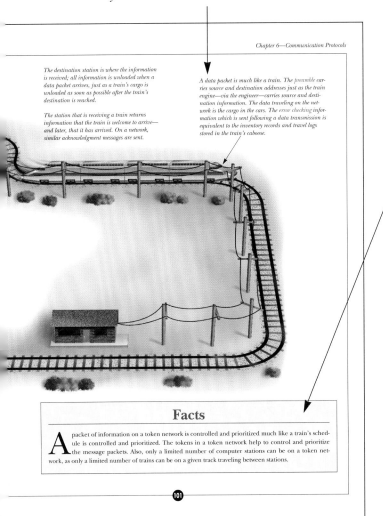

Chapter 6—Communication Protocols

The destination station is where the information is received; all information is unloaded when a data packet arrives, just as a train's cargo is unloaded as soon as possible after the train's destination is reached.

The station that is receiving a train returns information that the train is welcome to arrive—and later, that it has arrived. On a network, similar acknowledgment messages are sent.

A data packet is much like a train. The preamble carries source and destination addresses just as the train engine—via the engineer—carries source and destination information. The data traveling on the network is the cargo in the cars. The error checking information which is sent following a data transmission is equivalent to the inventory records and travel logs stored in the train's caboose.

Facts

A packet of information on a token network is controlled and prioritized much like a train's schedule is controlled and prioritized. The tokens in a token network help to control and prioritize the message packets. Also, only a limited number of computer stations can be on a token network, as only a limited number of trains can be on a given track traveling between stations.

101

This column is the Facts column. It provides specific information about the topic presented in the illustration(s). Specific information relating to manufacturing standards, industry trends, and slightly more technical explanations are presented here.

Facts

You see what I mean? You have been introduced to the book already, but the Facts column is a space where you can gain extra information. Not only might you find a more technical discussion or a look at particular products here, but you'll also notice some words and phrases appearing in a different color. This denotes that a word or phrase is new or difficult to grasp and is explained more thoroughly in a glossary entry. The glossary is located at the back of the book, and provides definitions and clarification of many terms associated with networking. Now, sit back and thoroughly enjoy *Networking Illustrated*.

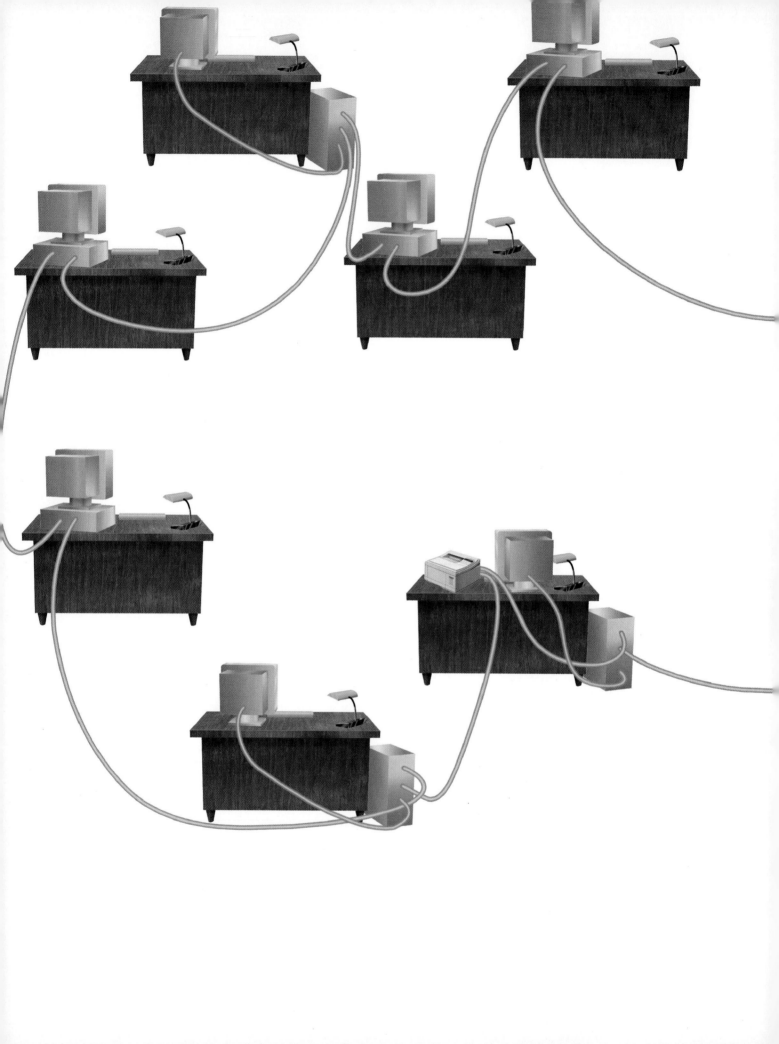

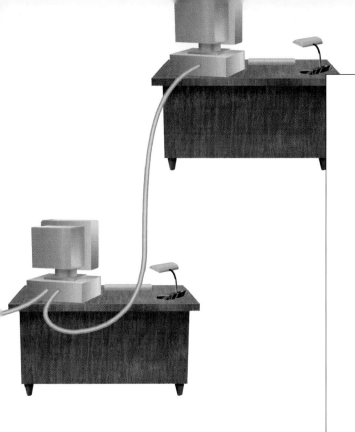

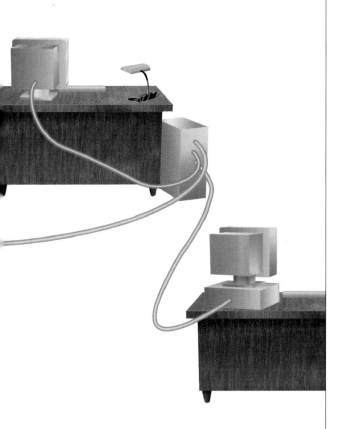

What Is a Network?

Sharing on a Network

A network is for sharing. Sharing files. Sharing printers. Sharing applications. All information on a network is sharable. This sharing helps to increase personal and workgroup productivity. Also, capital cost savings can be gained by sharing printers and devices, sharing software licenses, and better utilization of computing resources.

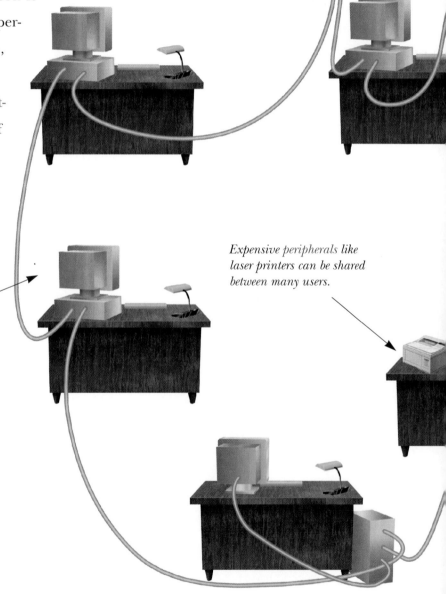

Expensive peripherals like laser printers can be shared between many users.

A workstation connected to the network makes shared devices and applications available to the user.

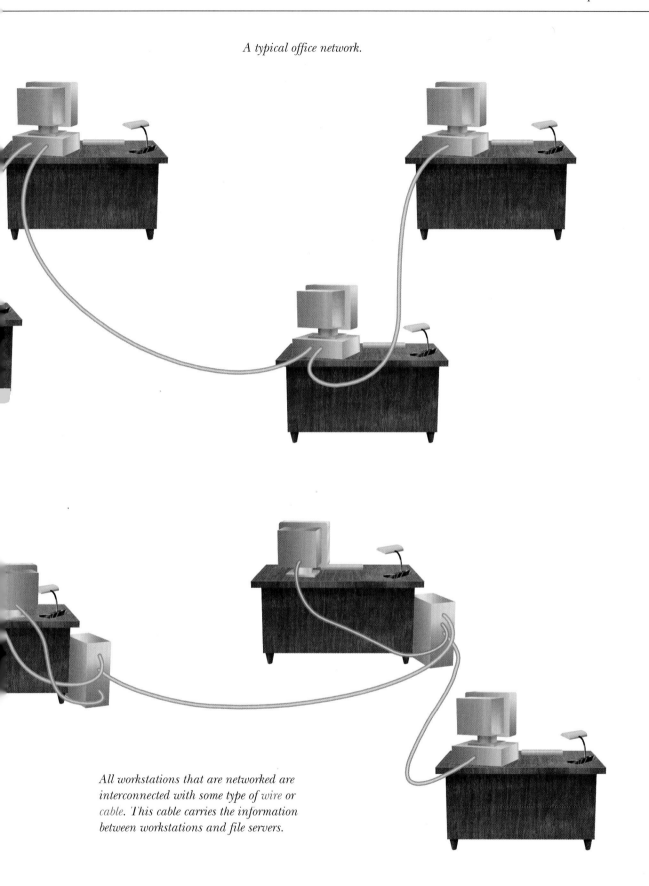

A typical office network.

All workstations that are networked are interconnected with some type of wire or cable. This cable carries the information between workstations and file servers.

A Basic Network

Anetwork basically consists of two or more devices that share information. It can be as complicated as several hundred workstations connected to file servers, minicomputers, and mainframes. Or, it can be as simple as two computers interconnected to share basic printers and files. A network provides the connection to share information, devices, files, and ideas.

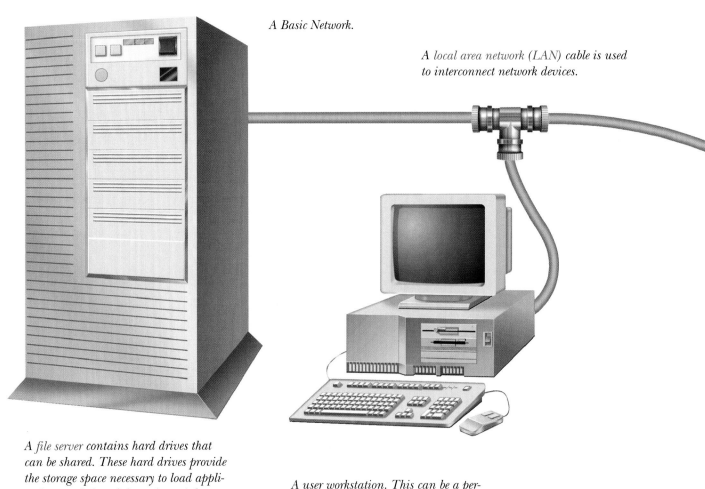

A Basic Network.

A local area network (LAN) cable is used to interconnect network devices.

A file server contains hard drives that can be shared. These hard drives provide the storage space necessary to load applications and shared data. A special program called a network operating system (NOS) is used to allocate these resources on a network.

A user workstation. This can be a personal computer, UNIX workstation, Macintosh, or any other individual computing resource.

Facts

Anetwork everyone uses is the telephone network. The telephone network allows many users to share a common resource—incoming and outgoing telephone lines. The telephone system is the most complex network in the world because the number of nodes (telephone sets) is in the millions. Yet we are at ease with the technology because everyone knows how to use it and does not even give the underlying technology a second thought. The network is in the background providing all the services necessary to connect your calls.

A computer network works the same way. Once a computer network is installed and set up, it works in the background providing the necessary services to connect workstations to shared resources.

A network device can be connected to the network to share peripherals. This network device may be a print server or terminal server. It provides the parallel and serial connection needed to connect modems and printers. It also contains special software that allows it to share devices on a network.

A printer or other peripheral is connected to the server, and becomes available to multiple users on the LAN.

Campus Network

Many organizations have a campus-like setup for their facilities. These facilities can be interconnected to allow computer users in each building to share information and resources. The links between the buildings are either above-ground cables or underground wires.

GOVERNMENT CENTER

A campus network got its name from college campuses. Colleges were among the first organizations to interconnect multiple buildings on a single network. Any company that has offices, factories, and warehouses in the same general area has a campus network. Major corporations that have several office buildings on a large property also have a campus network.

An administration or office facility can be interconnected to other offices and facilities. This allows the company management to obtain instant information about projects. Also, information can be sent to other facilities electronically in the form of electronic mail. This allows messages and requests to be processed rapidly and efficiently.

TO INTERNET

Companies and organizations may have many different facilities at a single location. These facilities are required to exchange information on a timely basis. For example, in a manufacturing environment, engineering may be able to send changes to production and correct a design problem. This would save money for the manufacturer by preventing product recall, service calls, or re-work. A computer network allows this timely information to be exchanged.

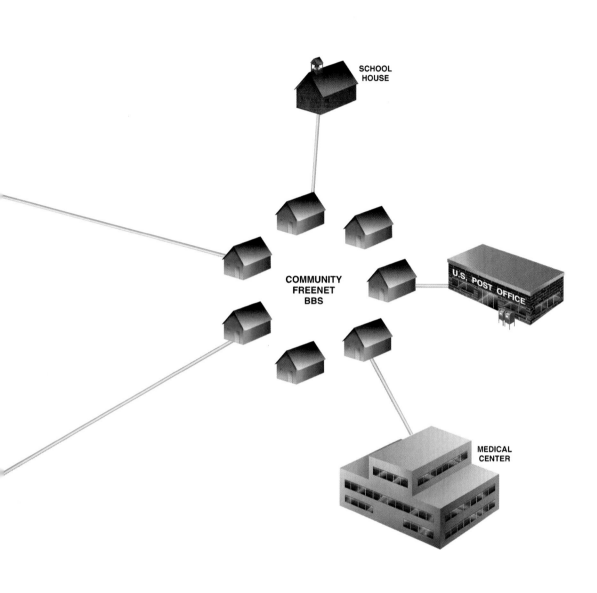

SCHOOL HOUSE

COMMUNITY FREENET BBS

U.S. POST OFFICE

MEDICAL CENTER

Facts

The interconnection between the facilities may be made using coaxial cable or fiber-optic cable. Routers, bridges, switches, and other network components are used to make the connections. These and other devices are discussed in later chapters.

National Network.

The wide-area links might be dedicated point-to-point T-1 lines, frame relay connections, or X.25 connections. Chapter 9, "MANs and WANs," provides a more detailed discussion of wide-area links.

National Network

Once an organization starts to share information and resources locally, it may become necessary to share information nationally to other offices. Networks can span company facilities, counties, cities, states, and the nation. These long-reaching networks are called metropolitan-area networks (MAN) or wide-area networks (WAN).

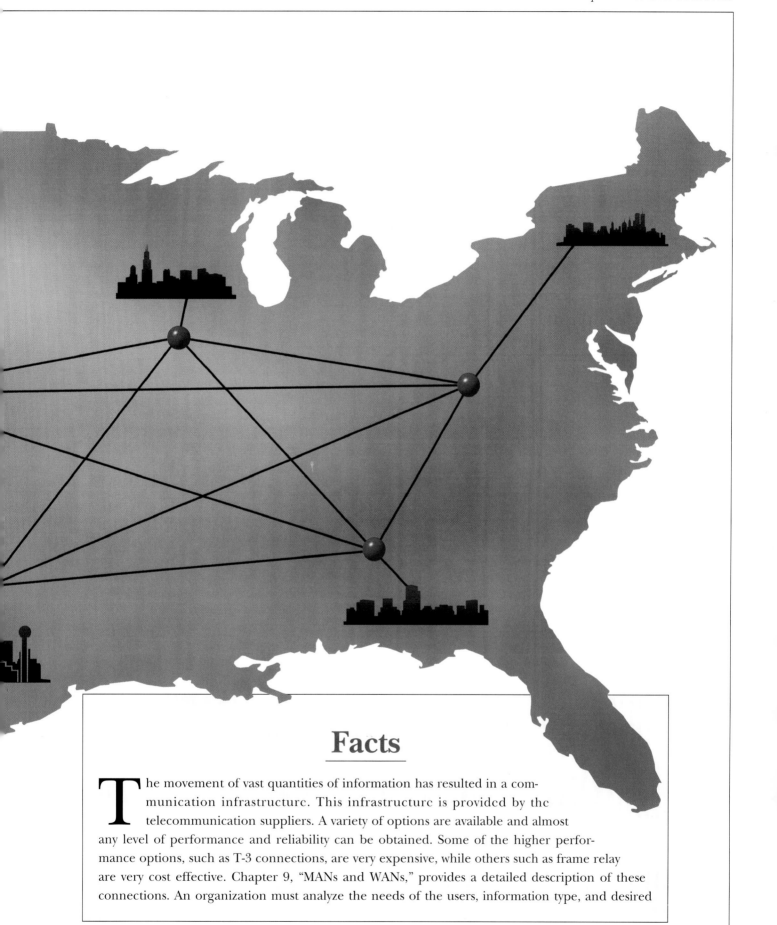

Facts

The movement of vast quantities of information has resulted in a communication infrastructure. This infrastructure is provided by the telecommunication suppliers. A variety of options are available and almost any level of performance and reliability can be obtained. Some of the higher performance options, such as T-3 connections, are very expensive, while others such as frame relay are very cost effective. Chapter 9, "MANs and WANs," provides a detailed description of these connections. An organization must analyze the needs of the users, information type, and desired

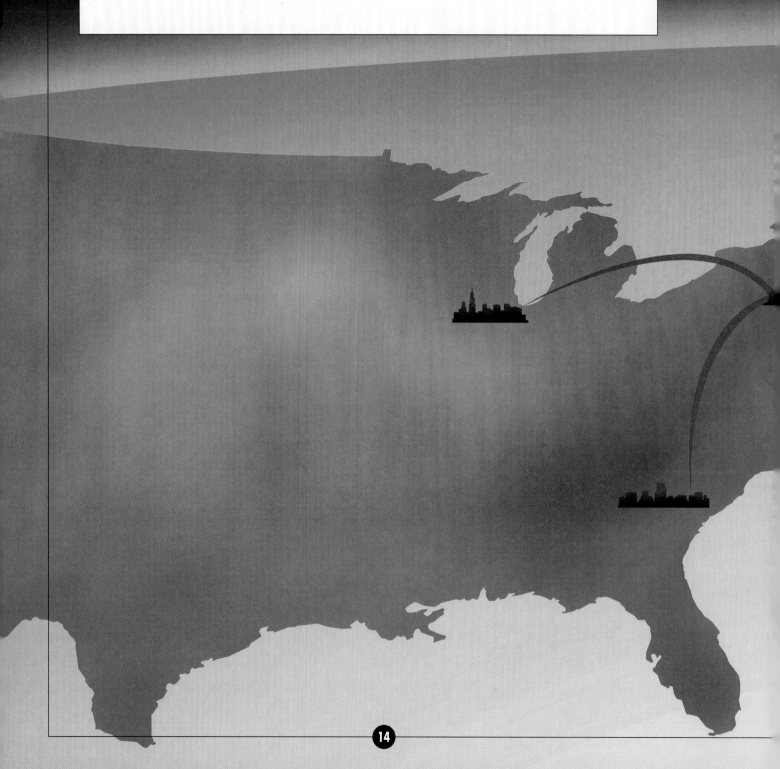

Facts

Networks between countries require the same level of hardware and software as do domestic long distance networks. Their devices are bridges, routers, multiplexers, and servers. These devices are discussed in Chapter 8, "Network-to-Network Connections," and Chapter 9, "MANs and WANs." These networking components are designed to communicate information between different networks, through different transmission media, and between different network protocols.

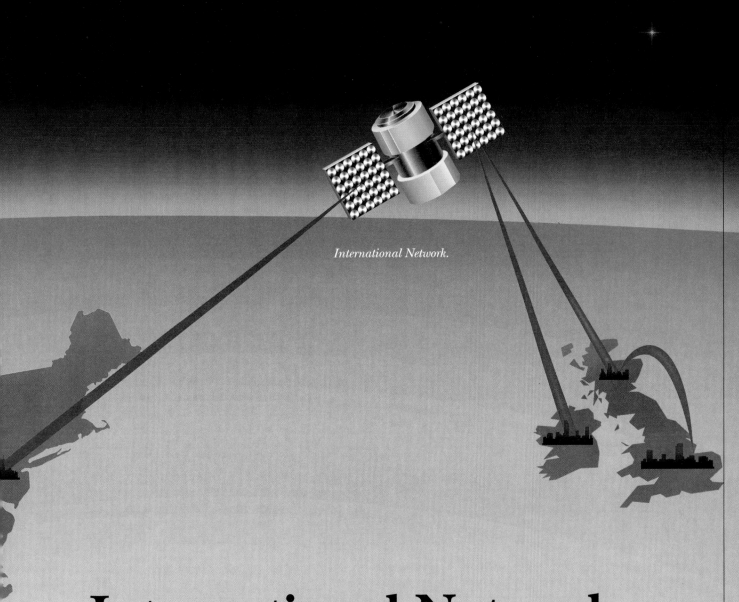

International Network.

International Network

When it becomes necessary to share information between different corporate entities in different countries, a whole new set of networking challenges comes into focus. Some of the challenges are based on performance, and others on cost and convenience. It is possible for a company to get a dedicated transoceanic cable to link facilities in one country to another. Other connections might be through satellite communications. Both of these methods provide reliable communication between countries.

Network Workstations

A network workstation is nothing more than a conventional personal computer with network hardware and client software added. Once a workstation has been properly configured and installed, the network operations are invisible to the user. The client software handles mapping of remote hard drives and directories to local drive designators, and redirects the output of the printer to network printers. The software also may redirect workstation devices to be shared with other users on the network or may allow workstations to use other devices on the network such as plotters, scanners, and modems.

The central processing unit (CPU) is the brain of the computer. Here is where programs are executed. Also, information is transferred by the CPU to memory and devices on the computer bus.

Inside a network workstation.

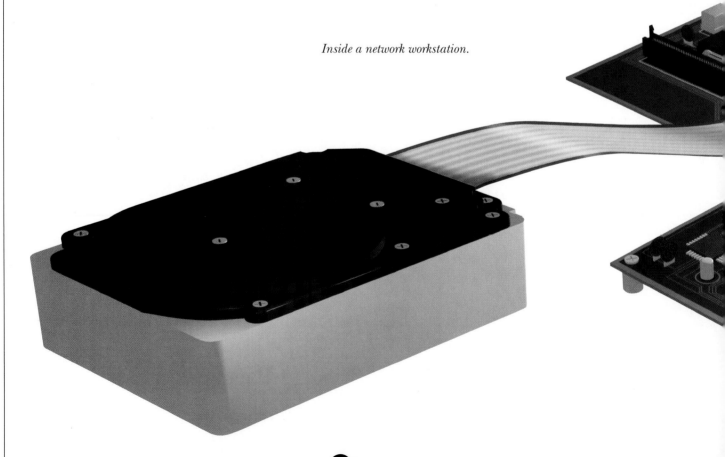

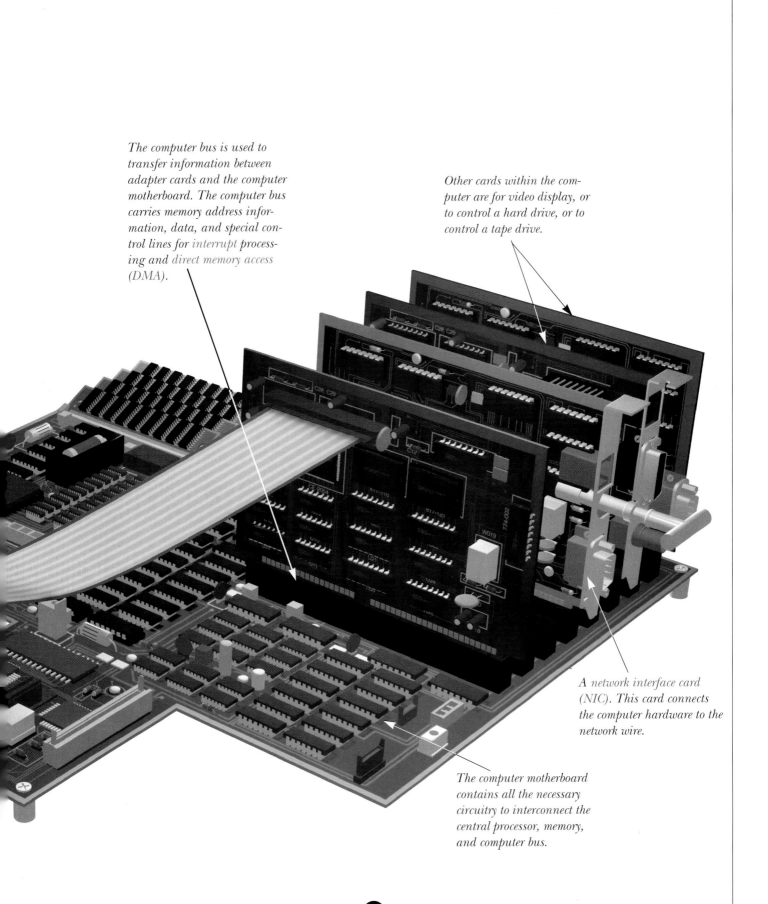

The computer bus is used to transfer information between adapter cards and the computer motherboard. The computer bus carries memory address information, data, and special control lines for *interrupt* processing and *direct memory access (DMA)*.

Other cards within the computer are for video display, or to control a hard drive, or to control a tape drive.

A *network interface card (NIC)*. This card connects the computer hardware to the network wire.

The computer motherboard contains all the necessary circuitry to interconnect the central processor, memory, and computer bus.

10,000 pages
53 megabytes

A stack of books might contain as many as 10,000 pages. The information on these typewritten pages could be as high as 53 megabytes. Converting this to data bits would give you 434,176,000 bits of information.

Networking Un-Illustrated Vol. 1

Networking Un-Illustrated Vol. 2

Networking Un-Illustrated Vol. 3

Networking Un-Illustrated Vol. 4

Networking Un-Illustrated Vol. 5

Networking Un-Illustrated Vol. 6

Networking Un-Illustrated Vol. 7

Networking Un-Illustrated Vol. 8

Networking Un-Illustrated Vol. 9

Networking Un-Illustrated Vol. 10

Networking Un-Illustrated Vol. 11

Networking Un-Illustrated Vol. 12

Networking Un-Illustrated Vol. 13

Networking Un-Illustrated Vol. 14

Networking Un-Illustrated Vol. 15

Data Transfer Rate

When information moves from the computer to a remote location, it is important to consider how much information will be moved and the speed that information can be moved. Once these are determined, a proper communication system can be designed and installed to transfer information. Information like computer aided drafting (CAD), drawings, and images require several hundred megabytes of storage. To transmit this information requires a network with a high line speed; otherwise it may take weeks just to send one image. On the other hand, a small document would not need a high-speed network to be transmitted.

Because data moves at a certain number of bits per second (bps), the time needed to send 434,176,000 bits of data would vary with the line speed. A typical modem sends data in the range of 2,400 bps to 14,400 bps. A local area network moves data from 1 mega bit per second (Mbps) to 100 Mbps. A wide-area connection can send data from 2,400 bps to over 65 Mbps.

24,000 bps	=	49 Hours
9,600 bps	=	12.2 Hours
56,000 bps	=	2.1 Hours
1,000,000 bps	=	6.87 Minutes
10,000,000 bps	=	41.25 Seconds
100,000,000 bps	=	4.125 Seconds
1,000,000,000 bps	=	0.4 Seconds

Facts

Once the volume of information is determined, it is necessary to determine the tolerable speed to transmit the data. Factors influencing this decision are cost of the line, cost of sending the data, and the timeliness of the data. Other factors to consider are the human factors, including how long a person will wait and how willing they will be to use a slow network.

Terminal Connections and Mainframes

Before the widespread use of personal computers and local area networks, computer terminals were connected to a central computer. This computer was either a minicomputer or a mainframe. These are still in existence and used with local area networks at many organizations. The LAN also can allow workstations to emulate a dumb terminal and to connect to these central repositories of information.

The mainframe or minicomputer is capable of supporting many different applications and hundreds of users. They usually have several gigabytes of disk storage, large tape drives, and high-speed communication channels.

The connection between the mainframe and the terminal is usually a serial connection. This connection may be direct or made through a device called a modem.

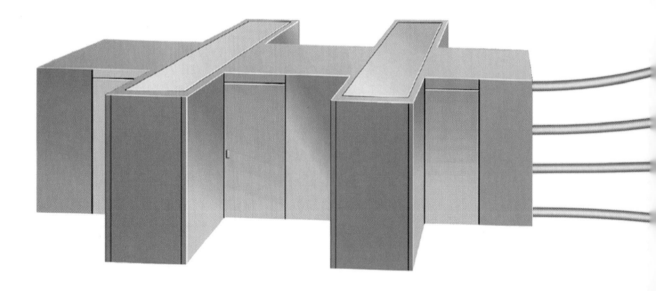

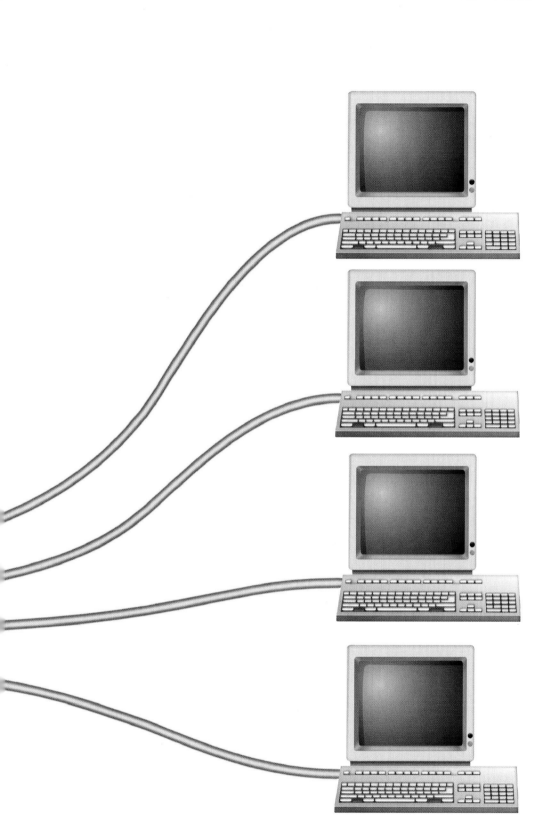

A dumb terminal is capable of sending information from the user to the mainframe host. It is called dumb since there are no local processing capabilities.

Terminal connection to a mainframe.

Character Sets

When computers were introduced, users communicated with the computer via wires and switches. This was complicated and time consuming, and a better communication method was needed. The preferred method of communication is through letters, digits, and symbols. In order to use these characters, a method of translating them into binary, which is the computer's native language, was needed. Several different encoding schemes were developed and are in use today. The most common of these is the ASCII character set.

Facts

The American Standard Code for Information Interchange (ASCII) uses a standard seven-bit code to represent characters and control characters. The first 27 codes are special control codes used to control communication synchronization and to send signals to communication devices. Some of these control characters tell the computer or terminal to backspace a character, ring the carriage bell, form feed, line feed, and so on. When this ASCII system was developed, the carriage bell was the bell on a teletype. Today it could be a computer speaker through which a tone is generated.

The next group of codes is common punctuation and special symbols. Then comes the standard digits (zero through nine), more punctuation and mathematical symbols, the uppercase letters, and finally the lowercase letters. Another standard for character encoding is the Extended Binary Coded Decimal Interchange Code (EBCDIC). This is primarily used on IBM mainframe computers.

ASCII Character Set.

Bits

Bits (4 3 2 1)	7	0	0	0	0	1	1	1	1
	6	0	0	1	1	0	0	1	1
	5	0	1	0	1	0	1	0	1
4 3 2 1									
0 0 0 0		NUL	DLE	SP	0	@	P	`	p
0 0 0 1		SOH	DC₁	!	1	A	Q	a	q
0 0 1 0		STX	DC₂	"	2	B	R	b	r
0 0 1 1		ETX	DC₃	#	3	C	S	c	s
0 1 0 0		EOT	DC₄	$	4	D	T	d	t
0 1 0 1		ENQ	NAK	%	5	E	U	e	u
0 1 1 0		ACK	SYN	&	6	F	V	f	v
0 1 1 1		BEL	ETB	'	7	G	W	g	w
1 0 0 0		BS	CAN	(	8	H	X	h	x
1 0 0 1		HT	EM	)	9	I	Y	i	y
1 0 1 0		LF	SUB	*	:	J	Z	j	z
1 0 1 1		VT	ESC	+	;	K	[	k	{
1 1 0 0		FF	FS	,	<	L	\	l	¦
1 1 0 1		CR	GS	-	=	M	]	m	}
1 1 1 0		SO	RS	.	>	N	^	n	~
1 1 1 1		SI	US	/	?	O	–	o	DEL

Practice the three steps to finding a character's ASCII value:

1. *Locate the character of interest. Use the letter 'A,' for example.*

2. *Obtain the upper 3 bits. The bit pattern for the letter 'A' is 100.*

3. *Obtain the lower 4 bits. The bit pattern for the letter 'A' is 0001.*

The complete code for the letter 'A' is 1000001, or in hexadecimal 41H, or in decimal 65.

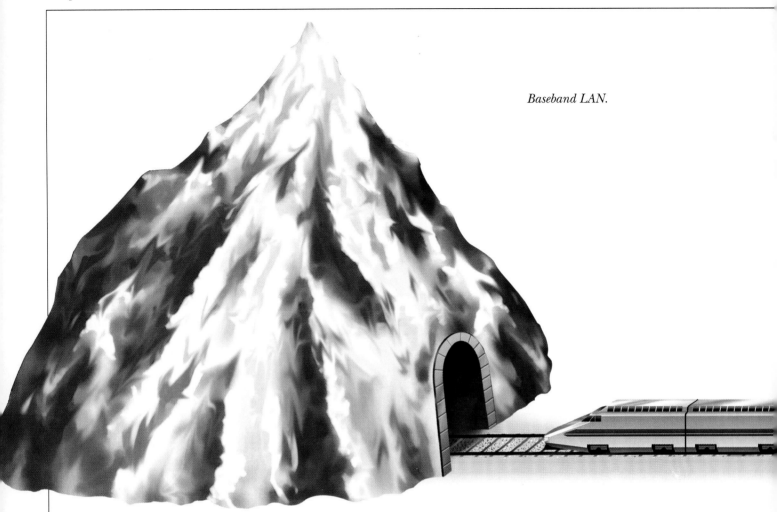

Baseband LAN.

Facts

The baseband LAN is probably the easiest LAN to get functioning and to maintain. Because this type of LAN technology is so easy to use, it is in use in most organizations. The popular EtherNet, ARCnet, and Token Ring networks all are baseband. The only limitation usually imposed on a baseband network is that video signals cannot be directly transmitted, because video signals are continuous signals. A continuous signal is referred to as an analog signal. A digital signal has two unique states: on and off. A baseband network sends digital signals, or analog signals that are converted to digital signals.

A baseband LAN sends data directly on the network cable. In many ways a baseband LAN is like a single train on a track going through a tunnel. The information is sent from only one workstation at a time. After the information is received by the receiving station, a new station can send information.

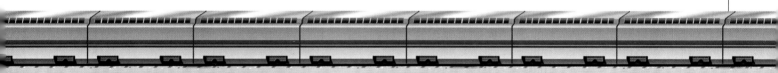

Baseband Network Communication

A network that does not modulate data is called baseband. Most of the common networking technologies in use today are baseband. A baseband network is like a single train track going into a tunnel—it only allows one train at a time through the tunnel.

Broadband network.

Facts

Abroadband network may be used to interconnect many different facilities. Since information is encoded onto a carrier wave, modems are required to change the digital information into analog information and then convert it back. This type of networking is usually more complex, but more flexible. A single cable can carry multiple channels of information, and that information can be analog. This allows voice, television, and computer data to be carried on the same network. Unlike a digital signal, which contains two unique states (on and off), analog information is a continuous time-dependent signal.

A broadband network can have multiple channels of information at a time over a single LAN cable, in the same way a wider tunnel can carry multiple trains.

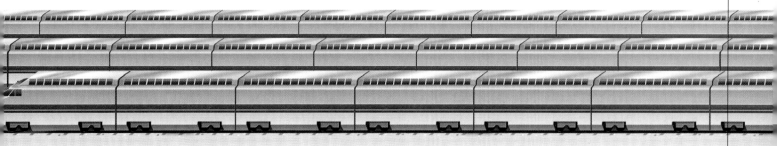

Broadband Network Communication

Abroadband network is like a train tunnel with several tracks. This type of network breaks the cable into multiple channels since the data that is being sent over the LAN is attached or modulated onto a carrier wave. Multiple carrier waves can be sent on the same cable. This is the type of network that is associated with cable television (CATV).

Video Conferencing

With the widespread use of computers and computer networks, the electronic organization is emerging. No longer are you required to wait a week for a letter to arrive—it can be sent electronically in a matter of minutes. Meetings also are changing. Through the use of teleconferencing, two or more groups can have a meeting in different and remote locations. The participants can see each other through television screens. Electronic whiteboards send information that at one time was only visible to the participants in a meeting. These and many other wonders are being attributed to data networks.

Video conferencing.

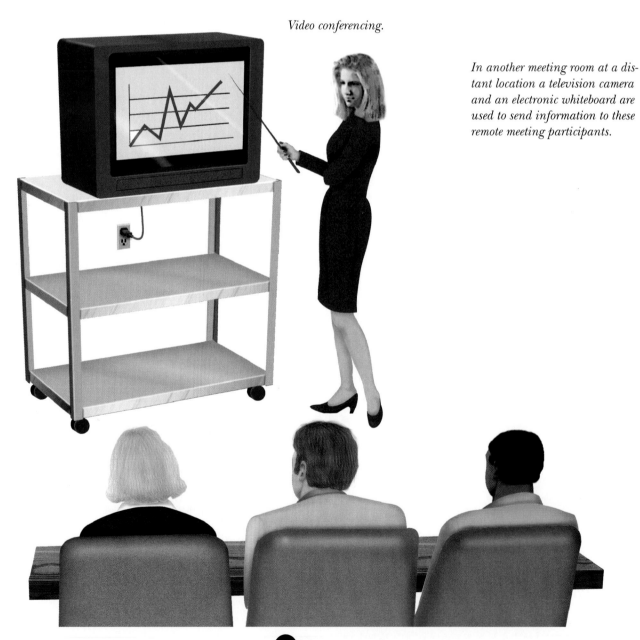

In another meeting room at a distant location a television camera and an electronic whiteboard are used to send information to these remote meeting participants.

Facts

As networks are expanded and data throughputs are increased, the number of electronic meetings that occur will increase. Today, only the largest corporations can afford this type of setup, but in the future most organizations and even our homes will have access to this technology.

The electronic whiteboard in the primary location is used to display a chart to other meeting participants who can't attend the "live" meeting.

A LAN or WAN connection shares information between the two remote meeting sites.

2

Basic Network Concepts

Saving through Device Sharing

There are many different reasons to install a network. One of the most compelling is to share devices. Some devices that can be shared are printers, plotters, and modems. Other items that are shared include application programs, hard disk storage, and hardware that performs backups.

A device called a print server connects directly to the LAN. This device makes printers and plotters accessible to workstations on the network.

Power 10BaseT Thinnet Parallel Serial

The LAN provides the media for workstations to share information and functionality.

Facts

By sharing network devices, an organization can achieve a cost savings because not as many devices are needed, and the ones that are available are more fully utilized. The drawbacks to device sharing are availability and performance. A device that is always being used might not be immediately available. This should be of little consequence for the end user at each workstation, as long as proper planning and consideration for others take place.

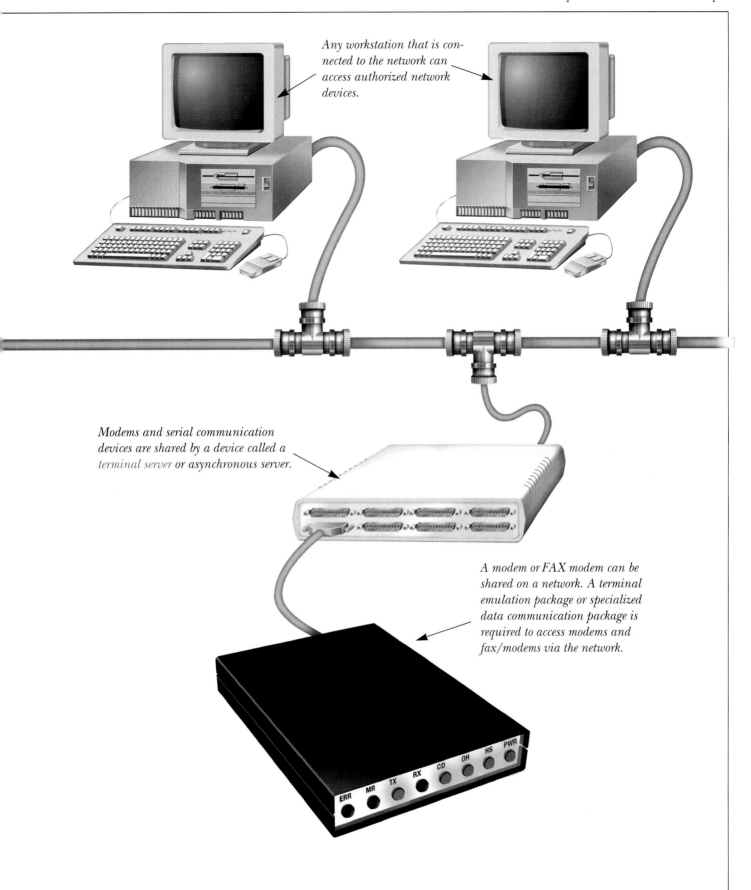

Any workstation that is connected to the network can access authorized network devices.

Modems and serial communication devices are shared by a device called a terminal server or asynchronous server.

A modem or FAX modem can be shared on a network. A terminal emulation package or specialized data communication package is required to access modems and fax/modems via the network.

File Server Login

Before a workstation can access remote file servers, a process must be initiated that creates a connection between a workstation and a file server. This process is the login process. During the login process, a connection is made between the remote file server and the local workstation. After user verification, remote drives to which that user should have access are identified and connected to the workstation. The remote drives appear to the user as local devices.

Facts

Depending on security assignments made by the file server, different areas of the disk drive may be accessible as separate local drives or directories. The authentication process allows the file server to secure information, and provides a method of controlling users and network access. The network administrator may set up special command files that execute locally on the workstations. These command files help the user to navigate the file server and the shared system resources.

The workstation user logs into the network using a special identifier called a username. A special access key called a password is used to verify the user to the workstation.

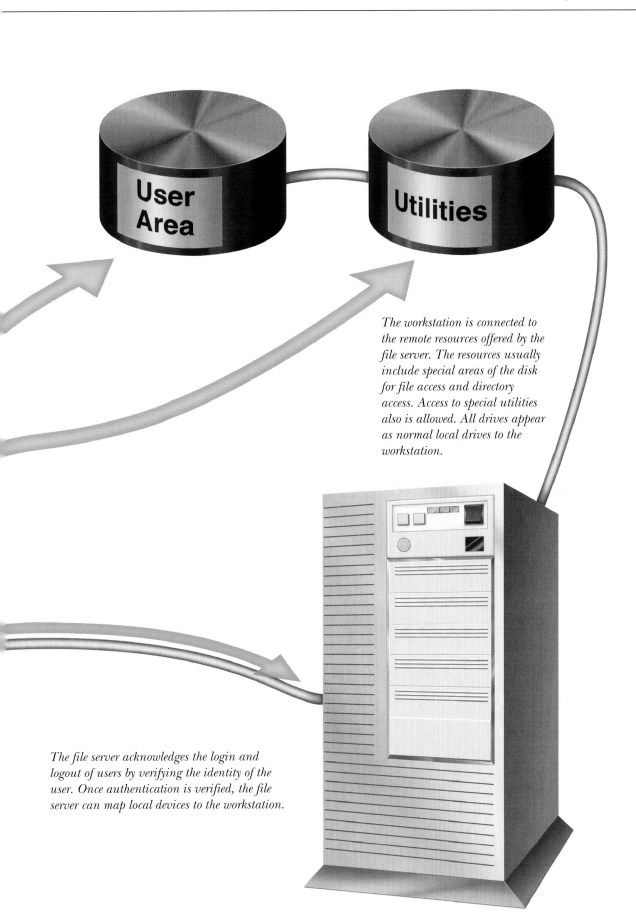

The workstation is connected to the remote resources offered by the file server. The resources usually include special areas of the disk for file access and directory access. Access to special utilities also is allowed. All drives appear as normal local drives to the workstation.

The file server acknowledges the login and logout of users by verifying the identity of the user. Once authentication is verified, the file server can map local devices to the workstation.

File Server Logout

After the user has finished a network session, the session should be broken or terminated. A special sequence of events occurs during logout. Because a logout is like exiting a theater, no user authentication is needed; however, authentication (showing your admission ticket again) is required for subsequent logins. The user usually enters a command for logout, and the file server breaks all network connections with that user and disconnects the user from all shared resources.

Facts

The logout process is much less complex than the login process. However, it is just as important. If a workstation does not log out of the network, network resources are vulnerable to misuse. Also, on networks where network connections or applications are licensed for a certain number of users, these programs may be kept inaccessible to others. On logout, these resources are freed to other users.

The workstation at logout time is disconnected from all shared network resources.

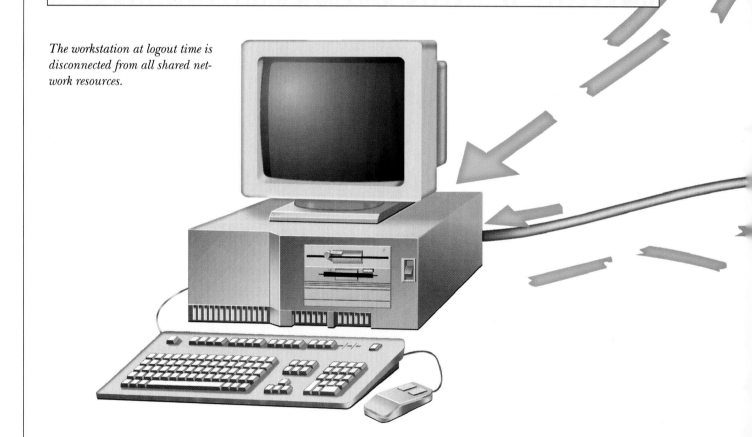

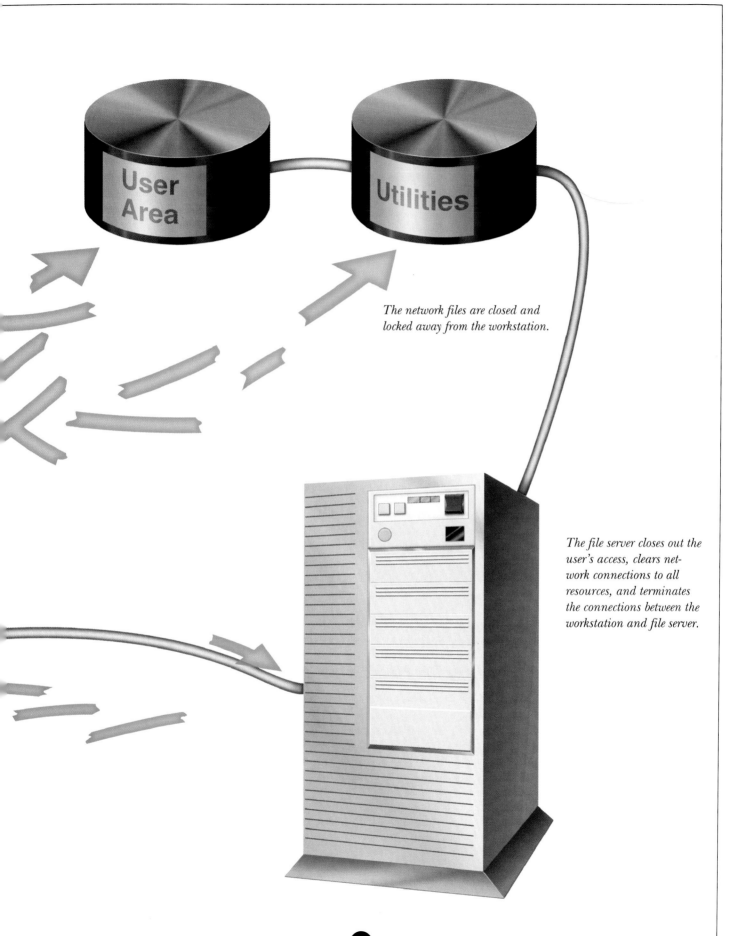

The network files are closed and locked away from the workstation.

The file server closes out the user's access, clears network connections to all resources, and terminates the connections between the workstation and file server.

Application Sharing

Networks also allow for the sharing of application programs. Each shared application program is installed from a networked workstation onto a shared network disk. Users are connected to the shared disk at login time, and then they can access and run whatever shared applications are on the disk.

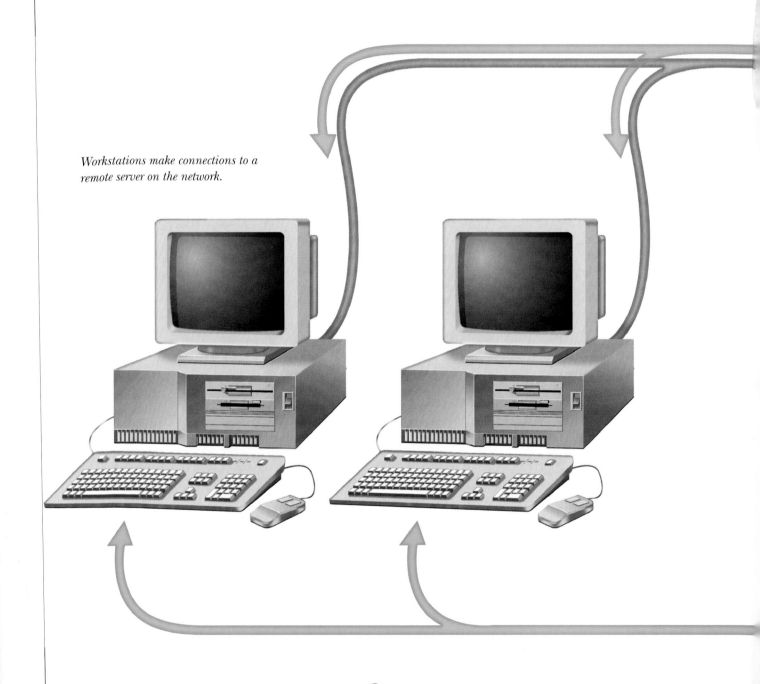

Workstations make connections to a remote server on the network.

Facts

Applications that are on a shared network disk reduce the support and installation problems associated with management on the workstation level. Without a network, each workstation must have its own license and installation of software applications. This is expensive and time-consuming.

An application on a network disk usually needs to be installed and configured only once. The network administrator then marks the application read-only and sharable. (See the following section, "Network File Access Methods," for more information.) When workstations connect to the shared drive, they use the network version of the program and store data on a separate network partition or on a local hard disk.

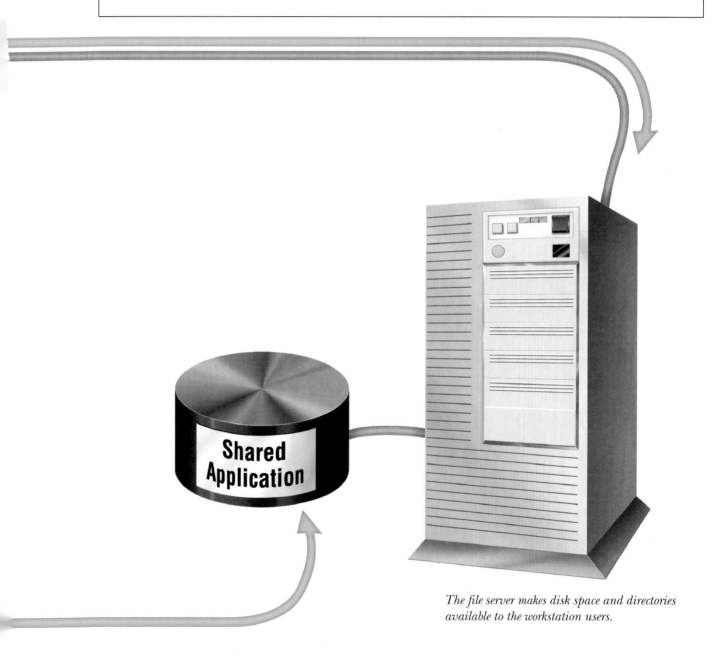

The file server makes disk space and directories available to the workstation users.

Network File Access Methods

A network controls how files are accessed. For many different users to access applications and other files, data file sharing is used. File sharing controls who can read and write a file, and exactly how a file can be concurrently accessed.

Is it really necessary to control file access? Think about some other situations where access is limited and it starts to make more sense. In a hospital, for instance, an operating room might be off-limits to all those who don't have clearance, or who show up without wearing scrubs and face masks; labs running blood tests might be off-limits to everyone except hematologists; the information desk and the gift shop probably can be visited by anyone, but visitor passes and change from the cash register aren't given out to everyone—only to visitors and customers, respectively. Controlled access is beneficial not only to preserve privacy and to prevent intentional wrongdoing, but also to make sure that everyone is allowed to go wherever they need to go, and that accidental errors don't occur.

To make sure no user on your network stumbles into the wrong place and knocks over a test tube, you should consider controlling access to data on various levels: you might restrict a user's access to entire drives, to certain directories, or only to individual files. Some software allows you to assign the same user different access rights for different areas within a single file. The following section, "Document Sharing," explains this concept further.

Facts

File sharing and file locks are used to control access to a file. The locking of a file is performed at the network operating system level. The actual locking of a file is transparent to the user. If a workstation tries to perform an illegal operation on a file, an error message is displayed.

Read-Write Access.

A file that needs to be accessed could be a document, spreadsheet, ASCII file, database file, or program.

These workstations can both read and write to the file. Usually only one workstation at a time can write to a file, although many can read a file.

Exclusive Write Access.

When a workstation (such as this one) opens the file for writing, all the other workstations can only read the file.

A file that is being exclusively written by a workstation cannot be accessed by any other workstations. This type of exclusive write is used when information must be changed and it's better for the information to be distributed only after it is updated. This is like putting a brick wall around the file that blocks out all users except one.

A workstation that is performing an exclusive write also can read a file.

Read-Only Access.

This workstation also would be blocked if it tried to write to the file.

The file open for read-only access can be read by many different workstations at once, but puts up a brick wall to all workstations attempting to write to the file.

Document Sharing

One of the many applications that a network allows is the sharing of data and documents. Sophisticated software allows for a file to be concurrently updated and distributed. This document sharing allows multiple people working on a project to update and share a document. The changes are available to all individuals as soon as they are committed by any user. Because all changes occur within the same document, an unambiguous history of changes can be tracked.

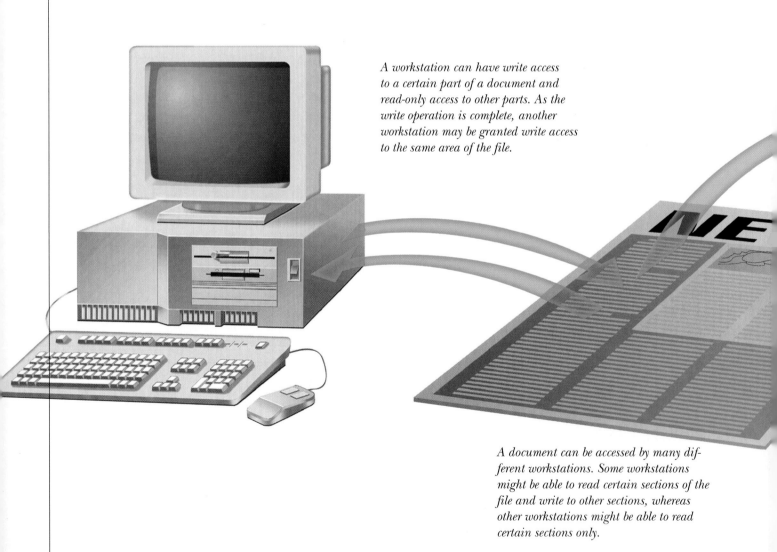

A workstation can have write access to a certain part of a document and read-only access to other parts. As the write operation is complete, another workstation may be granted write access to the same area of the file.

A document can be accessed by many different workstations. Some workstations might be able to read certain sections of the file and write to other sections, whereas other workstations might be able to read certain sections only.

Facts

Concurrent access to a file is not something new to networks. This type of access was allowed on minicomputers and mainframes. When information needs to be shared, updated, and accessed by many different individuals, some platform for sharing needs to exist. Without the capability to concurrently access a file, multiple versions are often propagated, with different copies of the document ending up containing different changes. To compile all the changes is a complex editing and revision task. With document sharing—since only one document is changed and updated—this editing and revision process is eliminated.

This workstation is able to read or write in the second part of the file and only read in the first part of the file.

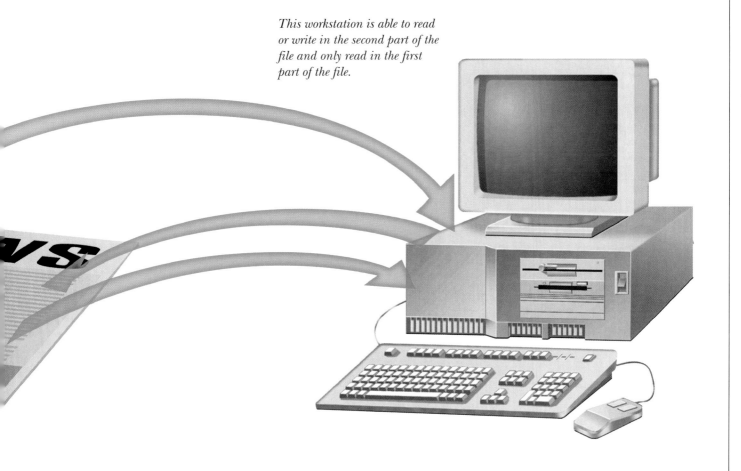

A shared data set can consist of spread-sheets, documents, databases, or E-mail. This information can be exchanged and updated concurrently by many users and many different workstations. The underlying software manages and tracks these changes for the user.

Workgroup Computing

Workgroup computing is a concept of the 1990s. It's based on the theory that all computers should work in a cohesive manner that allows information to be exchanged and updated. To perform this integration, a network must be in place, and then dedicated software such as Microsoft Windows for Workgroups or Lotus Notes needs to be installed. These products allow workstations to share their local desktops, send electronic mail, share worksheet data and cells, and access data sets simultaneously.

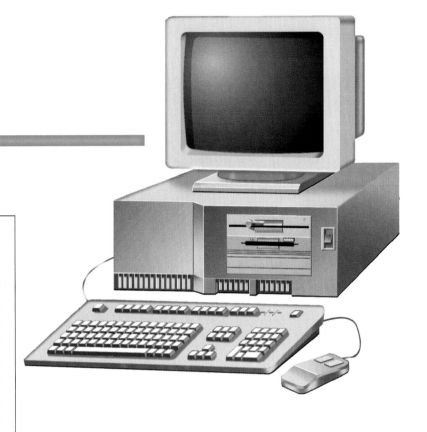

Facts

Because workgroup computing is a growing trend, and users need to share more and more information, it has become necessary to integrate these applications on the desktop. No longer is each workstation a single island of automation; instead, each is a cog in a vast information machine. This machine, driven by workgroup computing software, allows information to be cut and pasted with tremendous ease between desktops on different machines at different locations.

Electronic Mail

Exchanging information between computer users is the basis for a network. One of the most common types of information exchange is in the form of electronic mail (E-mail). E-mail can be found on most networks. The information that is exchanged is usually text based, but many E-mail packages include the capacity to attach files containing graphics, spreadsheets, or other application documents.

ADDRESSES

Workstations are like mailboxes waiting for information to be received or sent. You can transmit E-mail messages from computer-to-computer in-house, between network systems that are connected, or across CompuServe and other electronic networks or bulletin boards.

The network is the delivery person, usually in the form of wires. The network picks up and sends information between users. Depending on your setup, you may be able to download or upload files and programs across the network.

Facts

Electronic mail systems have been available on large computers for years. These types of systems facilitate communication between personnel and help users save time in sharing information.

E-mail also can be exchanged between companies and individuals using a public information service. Current E-mail systems allow attached documents to be sent. These attached documents may be text-based, binary, or even executable programs. Some E-mail systems offer users the ability to send and review spreadsheets, word-processing documents, and graphics. This allows for the mass dissemination of information within an organization.

When mail is received, an indication is sent to the user. This indication may be in the form of a change in the on-screen display, a pop-up dialog box, or through the computer's speaker in the form of a beep or little tune.

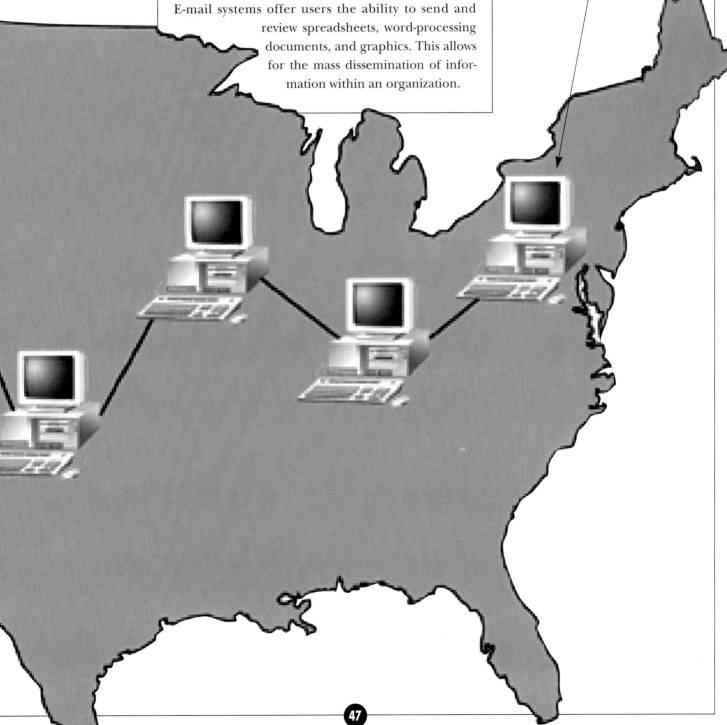

Network Security

Computer users have always been concerned with system security. Mainframes and mini-computers had built-in security systems that controlled user access to data and system resources. These security systems were like safe doors that could be opened and closed as needed. This all changed with personal computers.

A personal computer allowed more freedom and individual expression. No longer was the user locked out of data, applications, or system resources. Each user was free to use a machine—the entire machine—even if it was for only one application. However, this freedom started to cause problems. Vital information that needed to remain secret could be taken from a machine when the user was away, or information could be altered or destroyed.

Some products exist for providing security on single-user personal computers, but it's really networks that have added security to PCs. In a way, remote file servers are the mainframes of a distributed computing environment. File servers provide controlled access to confidential information. They prevent unauthorized access, and they protect the information in various ways.

Facts

Network security is a must for most organizations. In the past, a level of security from casual users was provided due to the complexity of systems. Today, with point-and-shoot desktops and extensive computer training and education, a casual user easily can gain access to restricted information. File servers are responsible for limiting this access. The login and logout process is one of the primary methods of access control for a file server. Other methods include file locking and file restrictions based on individual users or groups of users.

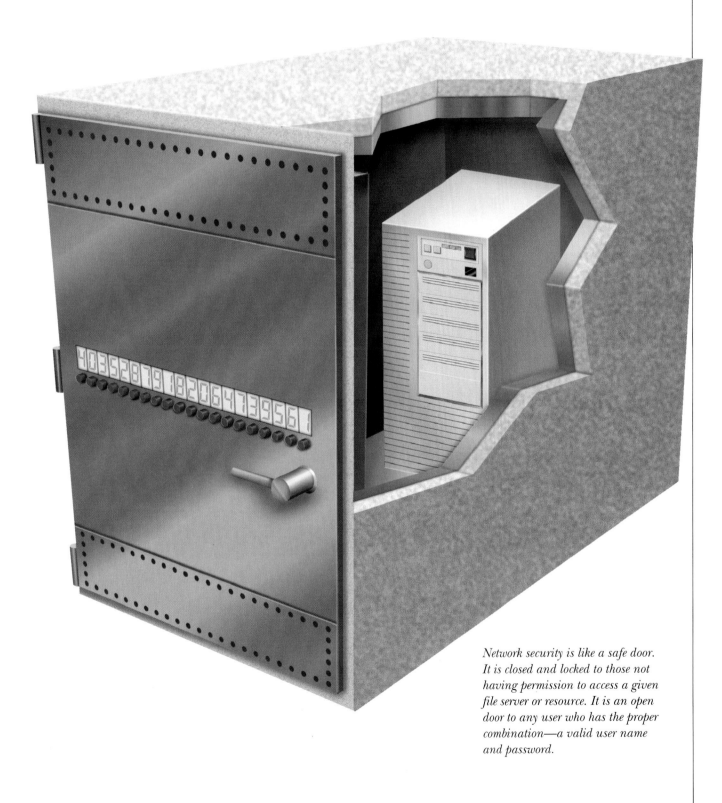

Network security is like a safe door. It is closed and locked to those not having permission to access a given file server or resource. It is an open door to any user who has the proper combination—a valid user name and password.

Virus Protection

One of the biggest problems with a personal computer in recent history has been in the area of computer viruses. A computer virus is a program that—when activated—destroys, disables, or annoys a workstation and the workstation's users.

Any computer or network file server, regardless of size, is vulnerable to a virus. A virus can attack a standalone computer or a networked computer.

A virus shield is like a fort wall— it is a barrier that protects a computer from viruses.

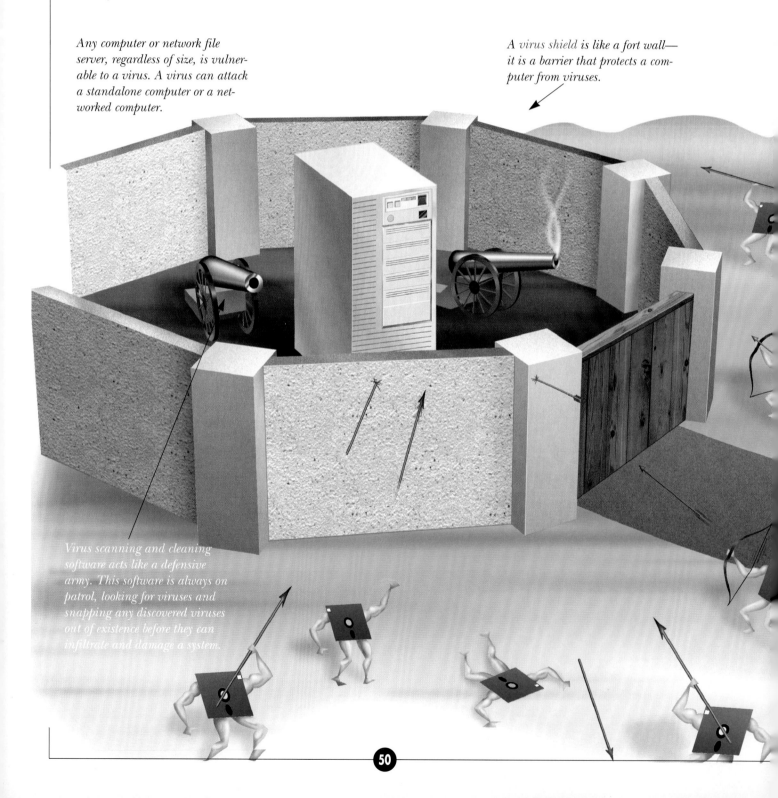

Virus scanning and cleaning software acts like a defensive army. This software is always on patrol, looking for viruses and snapping any discovered viruses out of existence before they can infiltrate and damage a system.

Facts

To protect a computer, you need to practice safe computing. The most common method of infection to computers is through an infected floppy disk. Never run an unknown program. Always use scanning software to check whether a strange disk contains a virus before using the software on your computer.

Install and use a good virus scanner. This software looks at each file and system section of a disk drive and memory for virus-identifying marks. If found, the virus is eliminated. Always use some type of resident virus-shielding software. This software displays a warning if it detects a virus invading your computer. If this happens, run the virus-cleaning software. It's also a good idea to make certain that disks you give to others are free from virus infection.

A computer virus is like an invading army—it needs to be stopped before it gets into a computer and contaminates the data.

Software Licensing

Computer software is licensed at purchase time. Generally, only a single copy of a program can be on a single computer at a time.

In a single-user environment, in order to have all the programs you want available on a certain computer, you must buy a copy of each program and install it on the single computer system. You end up with a well-equipped PC, but this can be extremely costly.

You learned earlier that hardware devices such as printers, scanners, and tape drives can be shared on a network. Fortunately, software also can be shared, as shown on the following pages.

Standalone PC loaded with all the goodies any user could want.

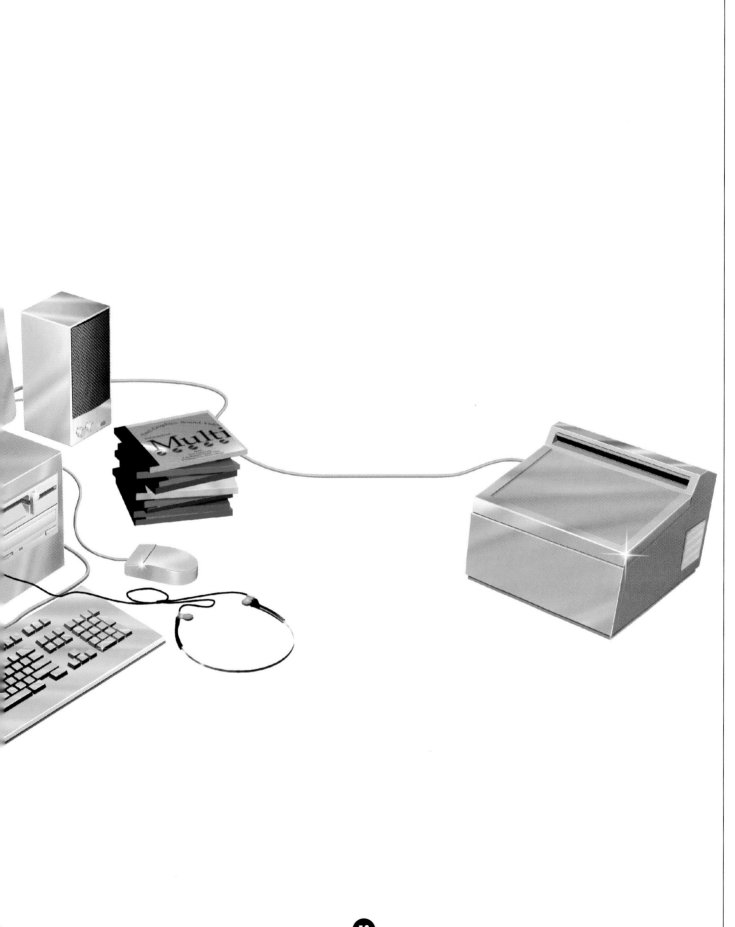

A standalone PC must have a separate license for each software application. Because only one program usually is run at a time, many other applications sit idly on the system. This sort of wastefulness can be greatly reduced by network licensing.

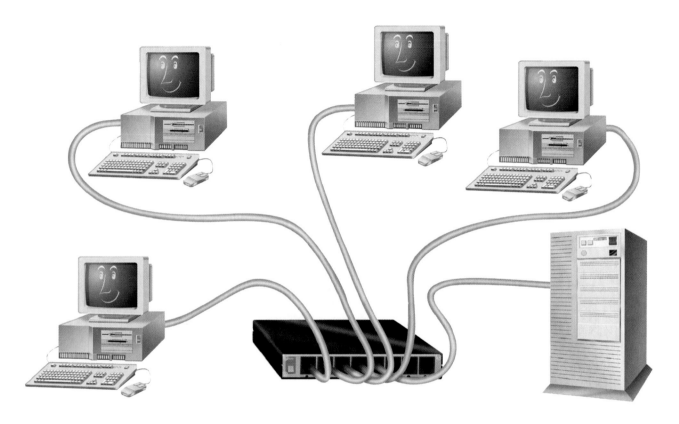

Block license.

A network application license usually is based on the number of users that a file server can support. Even though all users may be able to access the applications installed on the file server, the file server's own limit in turn limits the number of connections, and the software license for the application cannot be violated. Here, each workstation user can access the software. No one is locked out of the software, so evveryone is happy.

Facts

In a network environment, it is possible to buy a block license based on a file server's capacity, or to buy a metered license, sometimes called a user pack license. Metering and sharing software enables an organization to buy a few copies of software and share those copies among many users. This helps reduce software license cost and helps to get higher utilization out of each software license.

Some application software has a metering capability that limits the total number of concurrent accesses to equal the number of purchased license units. Additional users who want to access the application are locked out until someone exits the program.

Metered license.

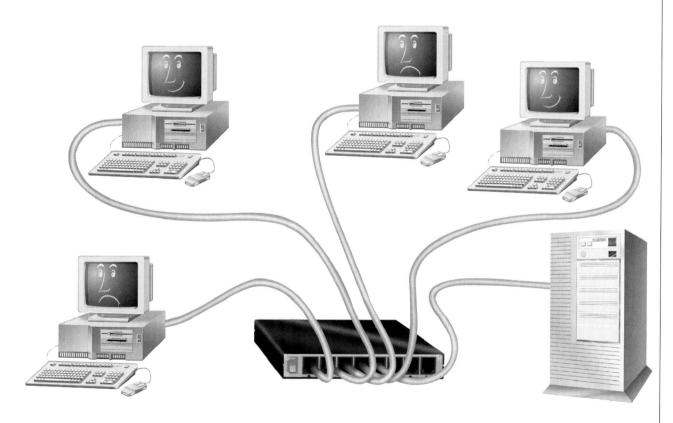

The application is stored on the file server, and a control file is used to limit the number of concurrent users. This control file contains the number of concurrent users and the total number of users available. In this example, the user limit is two, so the remaining networked users—even though they can access the shared application files—aren't allowed to run the application right now.

Network Accounting

I n many instances, it may be necessary to account for network resource utilization. This may be done to properly charge different departments within an organization, to track project cost, or to charge outside clients for network utilization. System resource accounting, usually handled by the NOS or additional software on the NOS, keeps track of used resources on an account-by-account basis.

Each network resource is assigned a cost. A different rate may be charged for each megabyte of disk space, each minute of connection time, each second of processing time, and each number or type of application executed.

As information about each item is collected, the usage is totaled. A report is issued detailing the total and unit cost of each item, and the responsible parties can be billed.

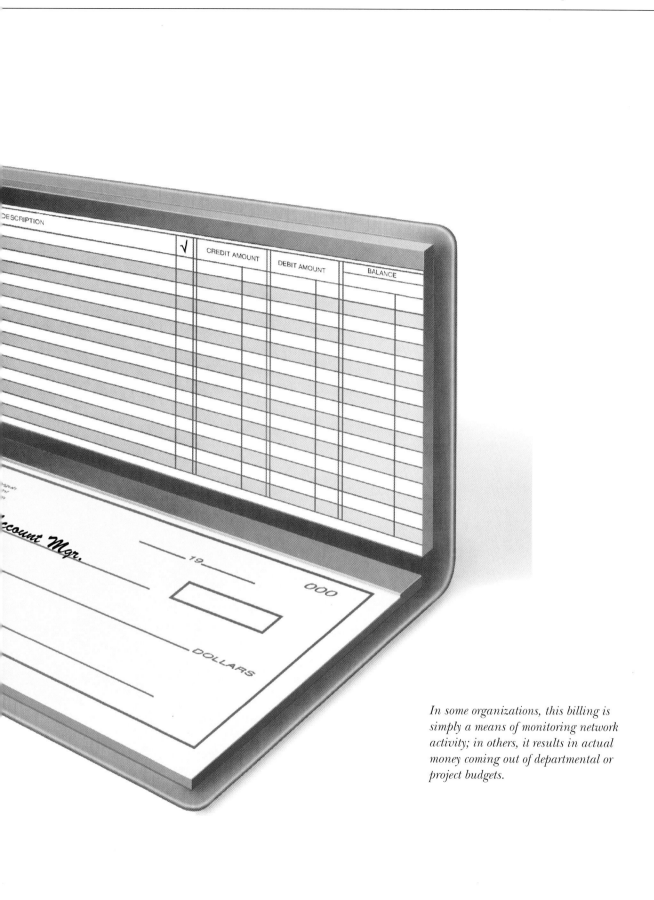

In some organizations, this billing is simply a means of monitoring network activity; in others, it results in actual money coming out of departmental or project budgets.

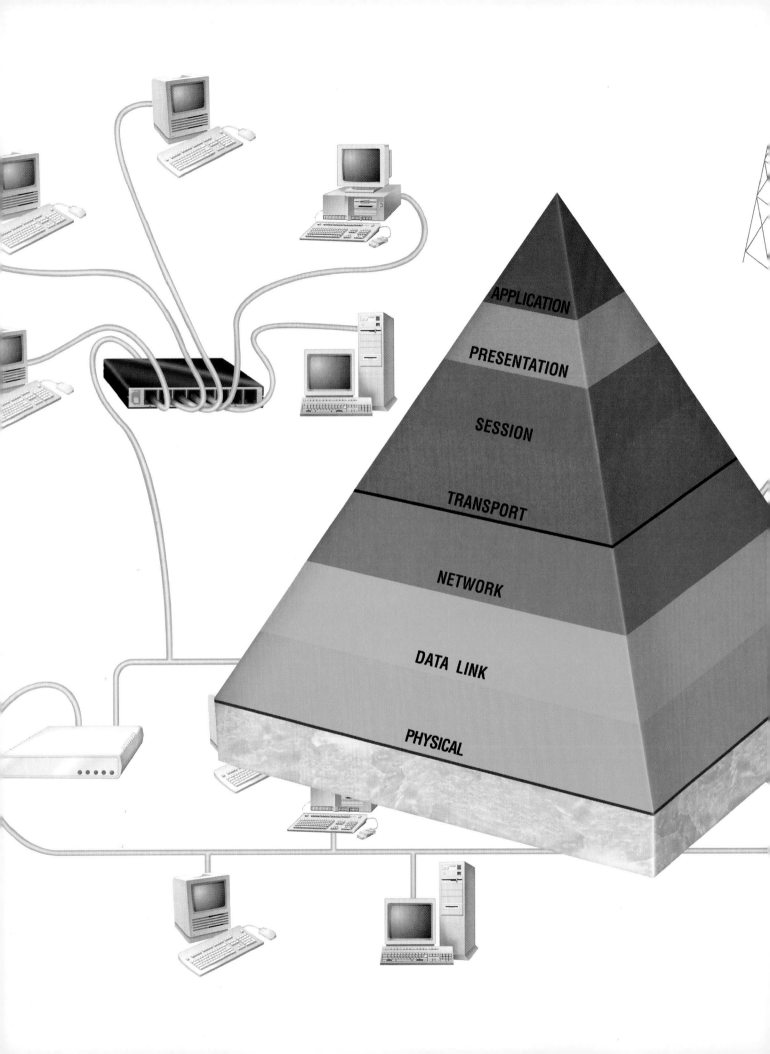

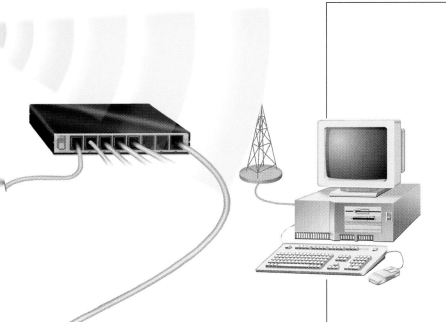

The OSI Model

Introduction to the OSI Model

OSI Host Layers

OSI Media Layers

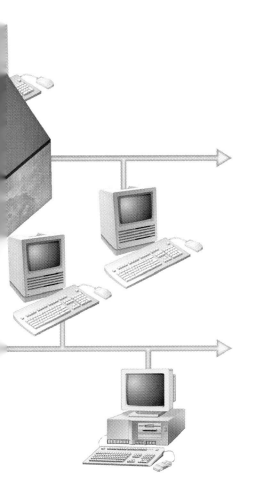

Introduction to the OSI Model

During the mid 1970s the International Standards Organization (ISO) formed a committee to develop a worldwide communication architecture. The OSI model is a standard for data communication that allows computer systems from different manufacturers to communicate. The Open System Interconnection (OSI) reference model was completed in 1980 and approved in 1983 by ISO in Europe and by the Institute of Electrical and Electronic Engineers (IEEE) in the United States. The OSI model is the basis for the majority of modern data communication protocols from various manufacturers.

Layers of the OSI reference model are designed to interface with adjacent layers. The Presentation Layer, for example, is designed to interface with the Application and Session layers. Each layer, however, handles distinct functions independent of all other layers, including adjacent layers. This allows for communication systems to be divided, and lets network architects design functionality into each layer to handle specific problems. Thus, the complexity of an entire communication system can be divided and addressed as simple procedures. The layering of a network architecture in this manner lends itself naturally to the division of functionality between multiple physical devices in a network design.

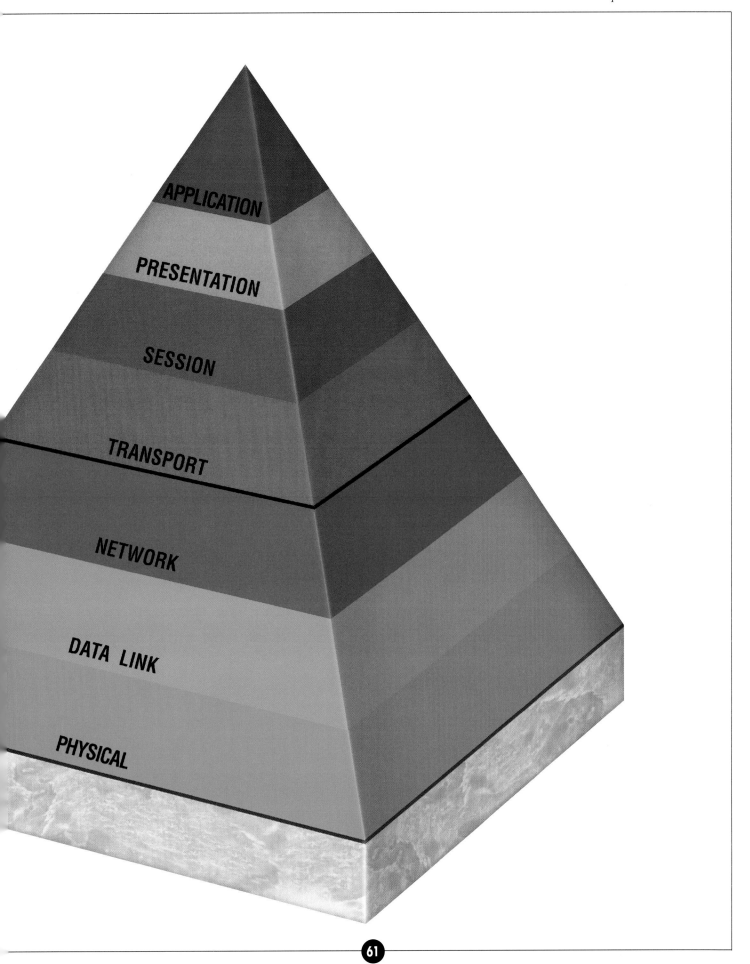

OSI Host Layers

The Application Layer, Presentation Layer, Session Layer, and Transport Layer comprise the host portion of the OSI model. These functions are usually present within a host computer, file server, intelligent bridge, router, gateway, or switches. Much like the construction of a pyramid, each layer of the OSI model is built upon underlying layers, with each layer providing services to the next higher layer. All layers taken together form a whole—in this case, a network. This divide-and-conquer approach allows for complex networks to be developed, in much the same way that a car is constructed on an assembly line or a house is built by laying a foundation, then framing, plumbing, wiring, and then putting up walls. If the designers and builders concentrate on their respective components, and have well-defined interfaces to each other, a complex entity can be designed and constructed. The upper four layers of the OSI model are designed to provide accurate data delivery between computers.

Application Layer
User interfaces are present at this layer. Some examples are the following: Microsoft Windows Program Manager, Motif, and OS/2 Presentation Manager. Many application programs also interface with the user and the network at this layer. These include common programs such as Lotus Notes, as well as electronic mail, word processors, and file transfer operations.

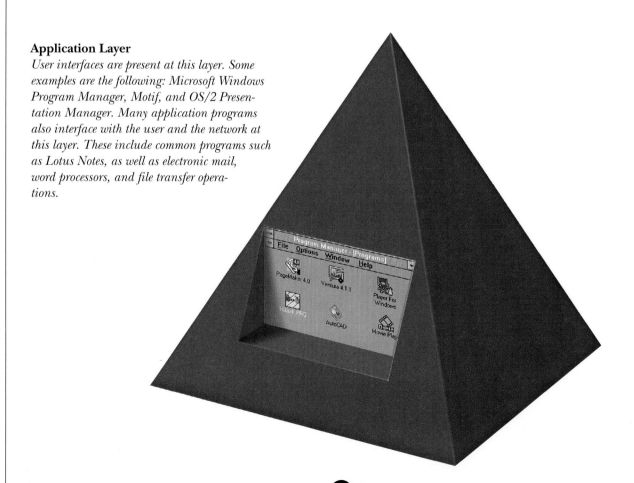

Presentation Layer

This layer is responsible for data format and translation of data from the Session Layer to the Application Layer. Other functions found in this layer are data encryption, data translation, and data compression. The data conversion format is left to the discretion of the communication designer, and all systems that exchange data must agree how the data will be formatted.

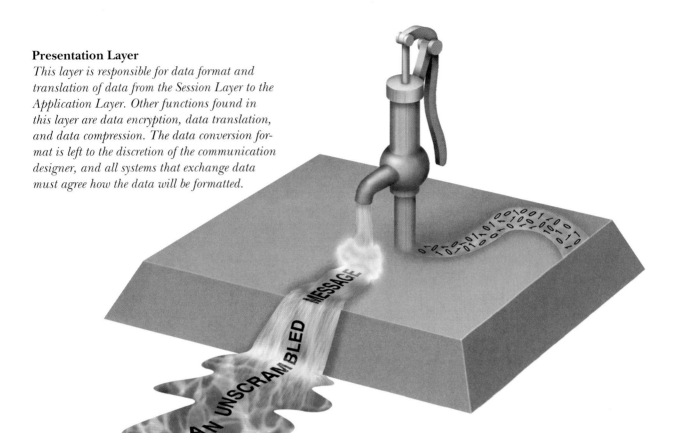

Facts

Throughout the remaining chapters of this book, you will occasionally notice the reappearance of a specific pyramid layer. The layer—or sometimes just the layer's color—is used to indicate on which level of the OSI model a certain networking hardware or software item operates.

Session Layer

This layer is responsible for error correction and for receiving data from the Transport Layer to be passed to the Presentation Layer. The functions found in this layer are error control, dialog control, and remote procedure calls (RPC). RPCs are programs that reside on a server and are called from an application program. The remote procedure call is used by Novell NetWare, Network File Systems (NFS), and other remote file systems. The errors detected by this layer are not communication media errors, but higher-level errors such as lack of disk space or the absence of paper on the printer.

NO ERROR

CONTINUE

Transport Layer

This layer is responsible for reliable delivery. In essence, this is the network's delivery service. Much like a delivery service tries to guarantee package delivery, the Transport Layer tries to guarantee data delivery. If a "package" of data, called a packet, is undeliverable, a message is sent to the requesting host that the message will be delayed. Among the methods used to guarantee delivery are acknowledgment messages, flow control, and the assignment of sequence numbers to data packets. A word of caution: This layer doesn't guarantee that a message was delivered correctly—only that it was delivered. To determine if a message needs to be corrected and re-sent is the responsibility of the Presentation and Session Layers.

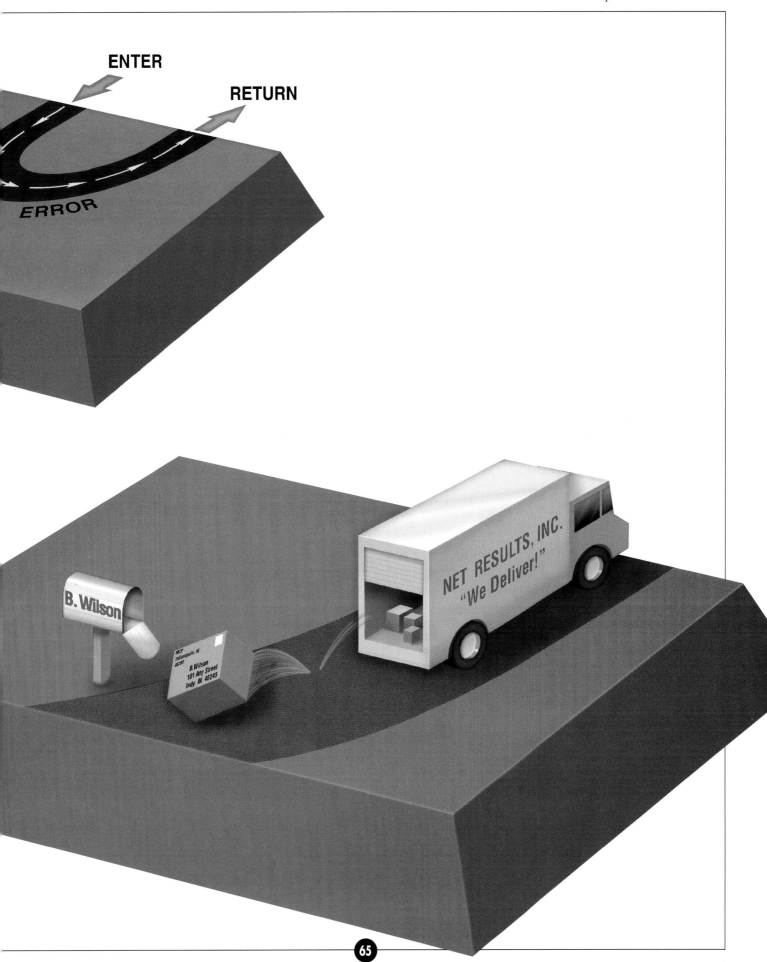

OSI Media Layers

The lower three layers are referred to as the media layers. These three layers—Network, Data Link, and Physical—are responsible for sending messages over the network. These layers control the physical delivery of the information, and usually are located collectively within the network interface card (NIC) or other device.

Network Layer

The Network Layer is responsible for placing information on the network. This is the layer that verifies and forwards messages based on the host address field. If an examined host is not the destination host, then the packet is forwarded onto a different network segment that contains a path to the destination host. The operation of message forwarding is related to routing—the process of finding the shortest and best path for a message to travel in order to reach its destination.

The information is transferred based on calculations that determine the best path for a message to follow. If the message is for the examined host, then the message is handed to the Transport Layer for further processing.

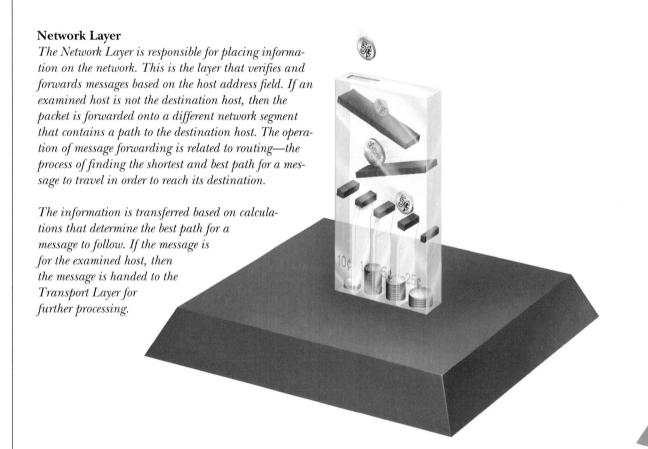

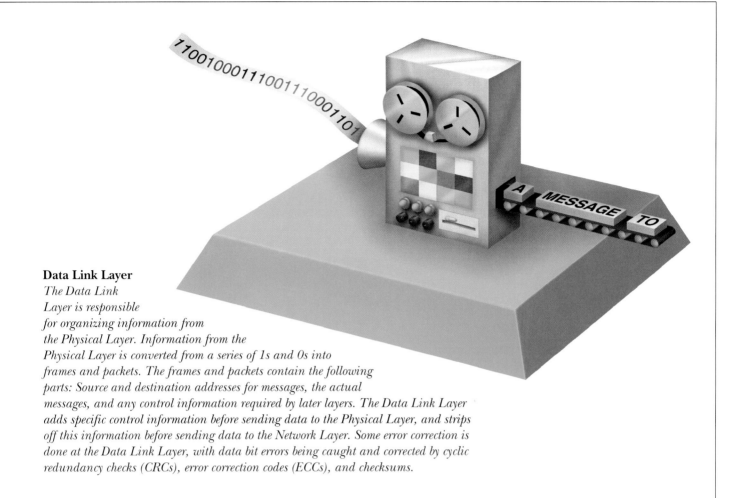

Data Link Layer

The Data Link Layer is responsible for organizing information from the Physical Layer. Information from the Physical Layer is converted from a series of 1s and 0s into frames and packets. The frames and packets contain the following parts: Source and destination addresses for messages, the actual messages, and any control information required by later layers. The Data Link Layer adds specific control information before sending data to the Physical Layer, and strips off this information before sending data to the Network Layer. Some error correction is done at the Data Link Layer, with data bit errors being caught and corrected by cyclic redundancy checks (CRCs), error correction codes (ECCs), and checksums.

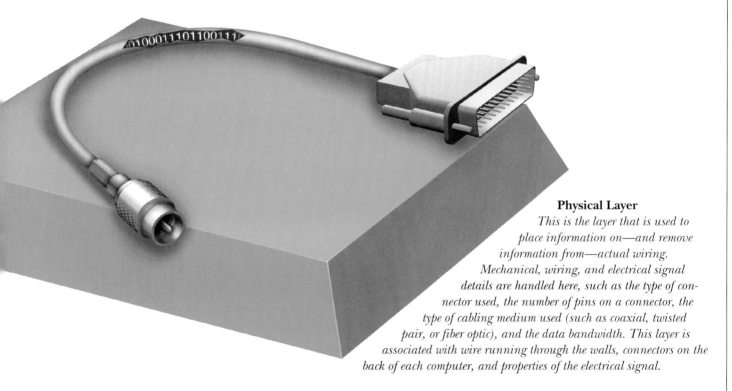

Physical Layer

This is the layer that is used to place information on—and remove information from—actual wiring. Mechanical, wiring, and electrical signal details are handled here, such as the type of connector used, the number of pins on a connector, the type of cabling medium used (such as coaxial, twisted pair, or fiber optic), and the data bandwidth. This layer is associated with wire running through the walls, connectors on the back of each computer, and properties of the electrical signal.

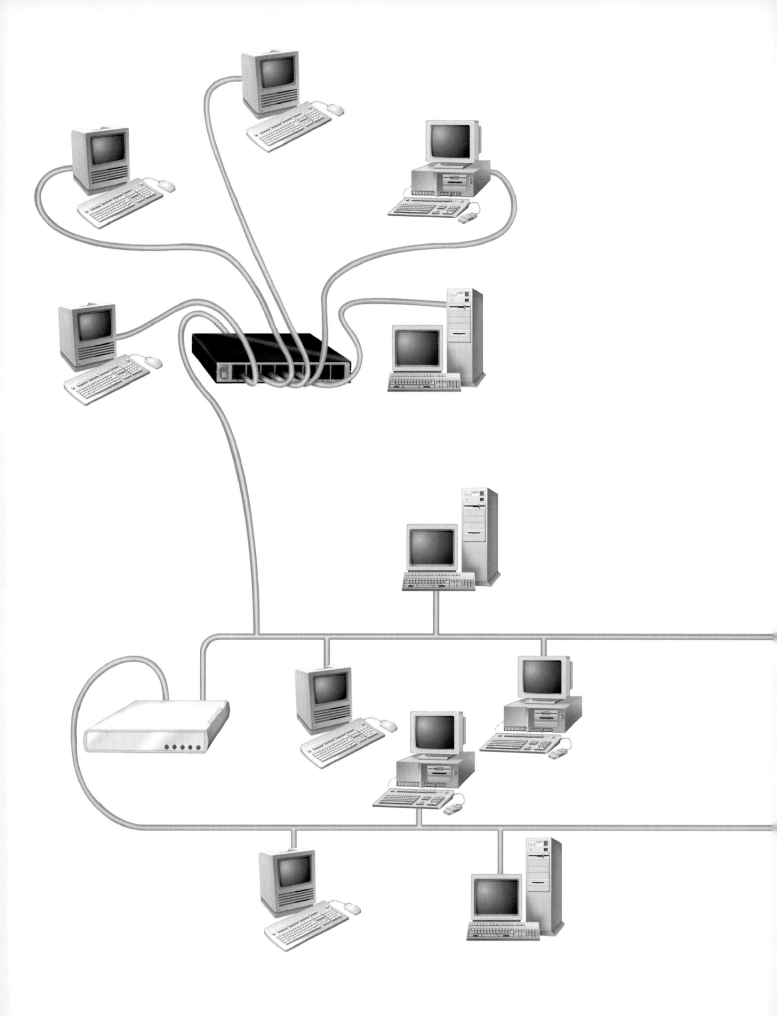

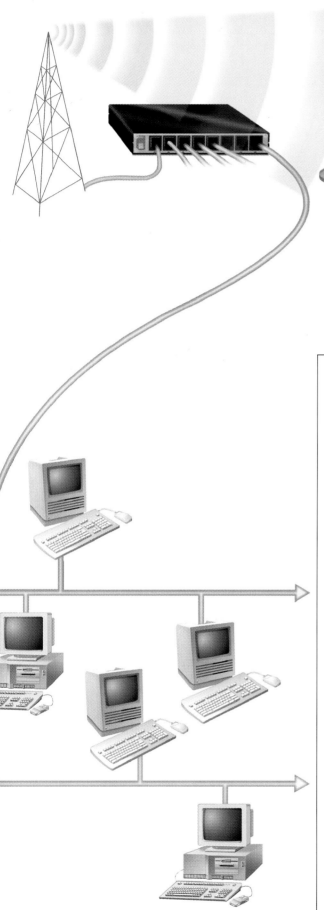

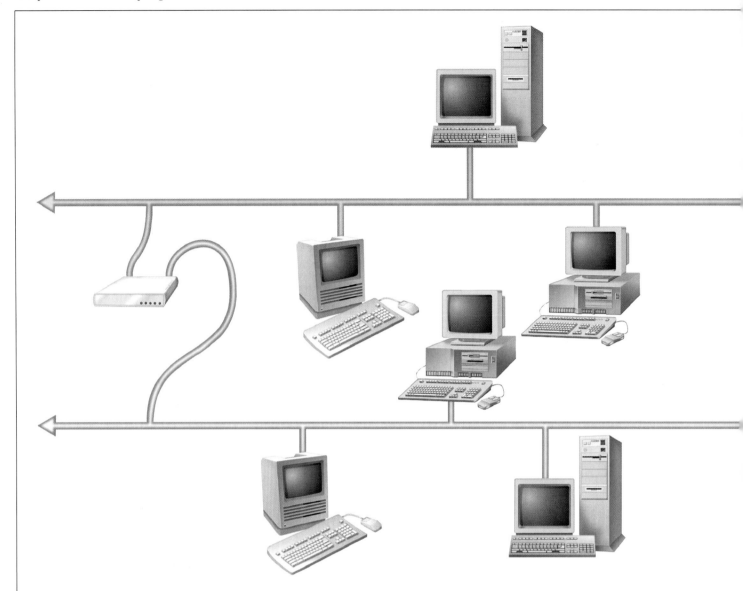

Bus Topology

A linear or bus topology attaches all workstations and network devices to a single physical medium. Each device is connected directly to a main cable that is usually referred to as the network backbone. The backbone interconnects each device on the network and also connects to other networks.

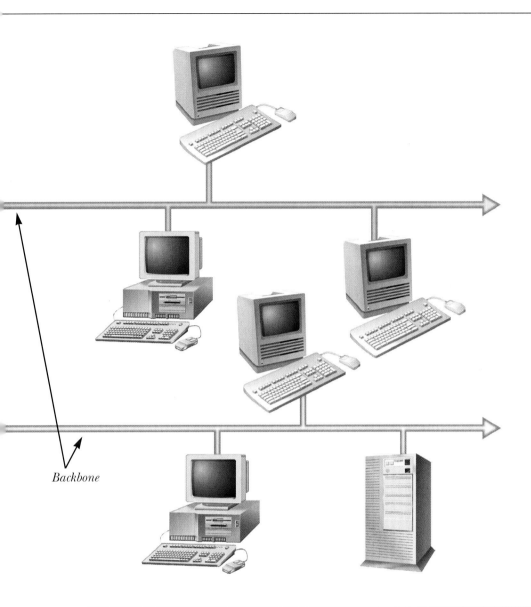

Backbone

Facts

The bus topology is one of the least expensive network technologies available. The cost depends on what hardware is used, who installs the cable, and other factors. Examples of bus networks are Token bus, 10BASE2 EtherNet, and 10BASE5 EtherNet.

To establish a simple network, all you need is cable and a network interface card (NIC). There is no requirement for other networking hardware to interconnect network devices. The only special requirement of a network is that the cable have electrical termination at each end.

However, there is a penalty for simplicity: an increase in the difficulty of troubleshooting. To determine where a network failure resides, you must disconnect and reconnect devices to determine if the failure is within a particular network interface card. Cabling also is difficult to troubleshoot because a single cable interconnects all the devices.

Star Topology

A star network connects each workstation or network device to a central point, much like a telephone network. In the telephone network, each telephone number is assigned a certain pair of wires that come from the central office to the telephone set. This pair of wires, or cable pair, is uniquely assigned to a certain phone number. Even though your telephone is connected only with the central office, that office is responsible for interconnecting your phone with the rest of the world. In much the same way, a central point called a hub, concentrator, or repeater is used to interconnect workstations on the same hub or on different hubs.

Facts

A star network is easier to troubleshoot than most other topologies because each workstation is isolated to a single cable connected to a single port on a hub. By simple substitution of cables and workstations, it is easy to determine if a network failure is on the hub port, the cable, or the workstation's network interface card. Another advantage is traffic isolation: Because similar applications can be grouped together on a hub, inter-hub traffic can be reduced. On the downside, a star topology can require more cable and, because hubs can have other hubs connected to them, a single hub failure can disable large parts of the network.

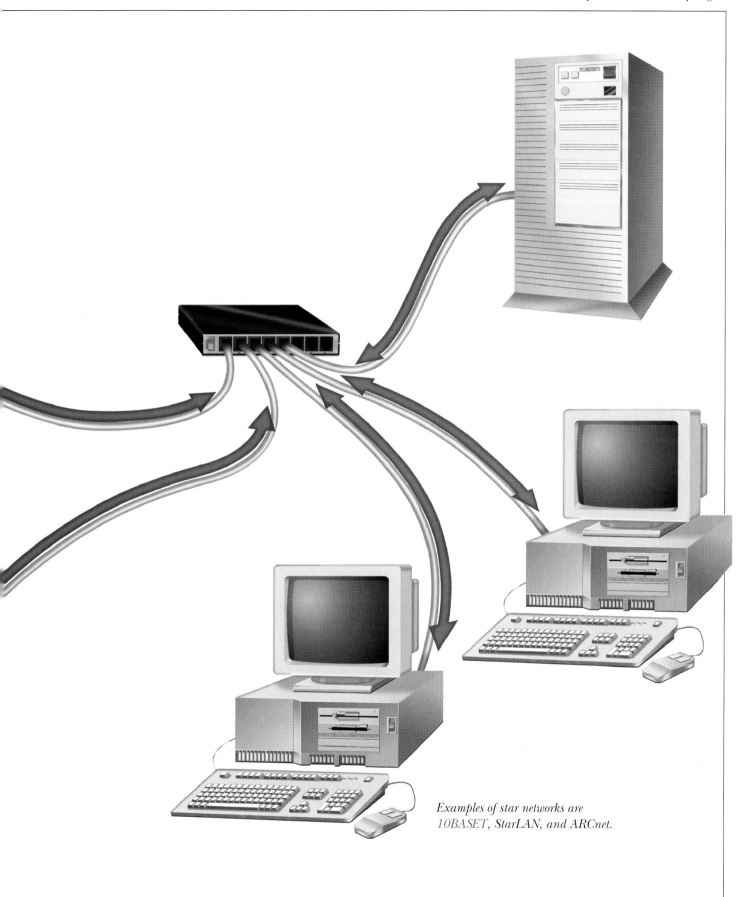

Examples of star networks are 10BASET, StarLAN, and ARCnet.

Wiring with Efficiency

Making a Mesh

A mesh network configuration was one of the first networking topologies used. To interconnect a computer, a separate network interface card was required for each adjacent computer. Also, cables were run between each computer. This topology is still in use today, but only for specialized applications and systems requiring extreme reliability.

The mesh topology is used to provide a reliable connection between computers. Since each computer has complete access to the communication channel, information delivery is predictable. This is important in real-time and mission-critical systems. Among the major drawbacks of mesh networks are the amount of cable required to interconnect all the computers, and the additional hardware (such as NICs) required to interface to the network.

A modern use for mesh networks is to interconnect networks from different facilities without routing information through intermediate systems. This would be used if the connections between all facilities were critical and if the failure of a single link could cause failure in the whole network.

The wiring associated with any network can become a spaghetti jungle if not properly installed and connected. This is especially true of a mesh network.

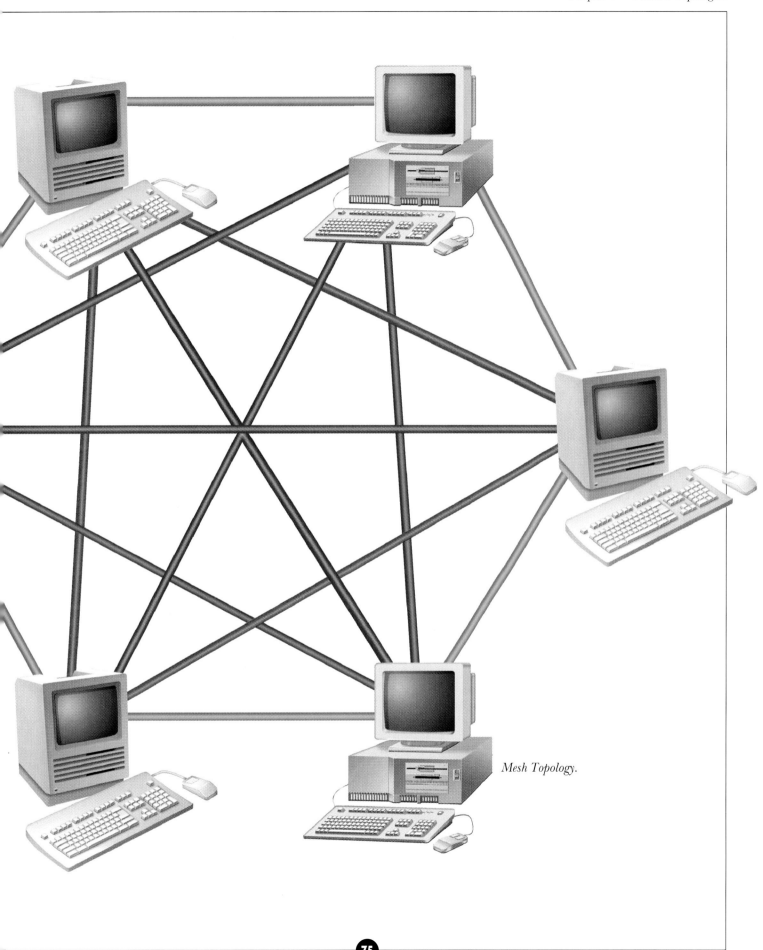

Mesh Topology.

Organizing the Mesh

A wiring methodology using wire racks and patch panels helps resolve the spaghetti jungle problem. Networks are made up of wire, connections, and devices. One of the most important aspects of network management is cable management, the process of keeping wires, cables, connectors, and patch panels organized and identified. Since most network problems are traceable to wiring and connection problems it is imperative that order be imposed.

One of the methods of organizing and connecting twisted pair cable is a punch-down block. These blocks are the same as—or very similar to—punch-down blocks used on a telephone network. A wire is connected to the block by using a special tool which pushes the wire through the connectors on the block. These connectors are spring-loaded and can slice the wire's insulation to make positive contact with the wire. Some punch-down blocks have RJ-45 connectors which can have cables installed; these cables are routed to patch panels or hubs as needed.

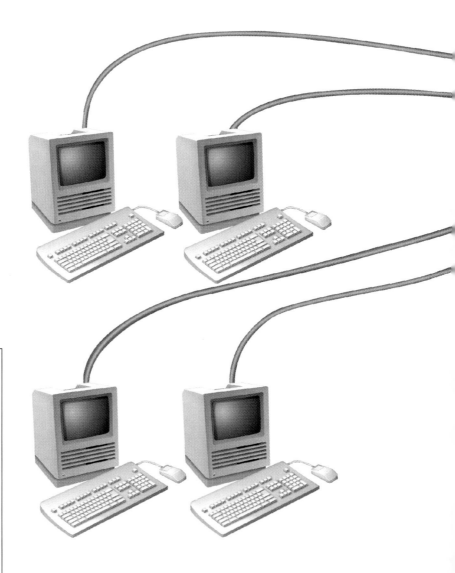

Facts

Cable management includes more than just patch panels and wiring closets. To properly manage your wires, you must label them carefully. Each cable must be labeled with a unique identification mark at both ends. This facilitates the job of a technician tracing wiring connections and problems between workstations, hubs, and other network devices. Clearly labeled cables and a drawing of your facility that indicates the locations of all cables help reduce network down-time.

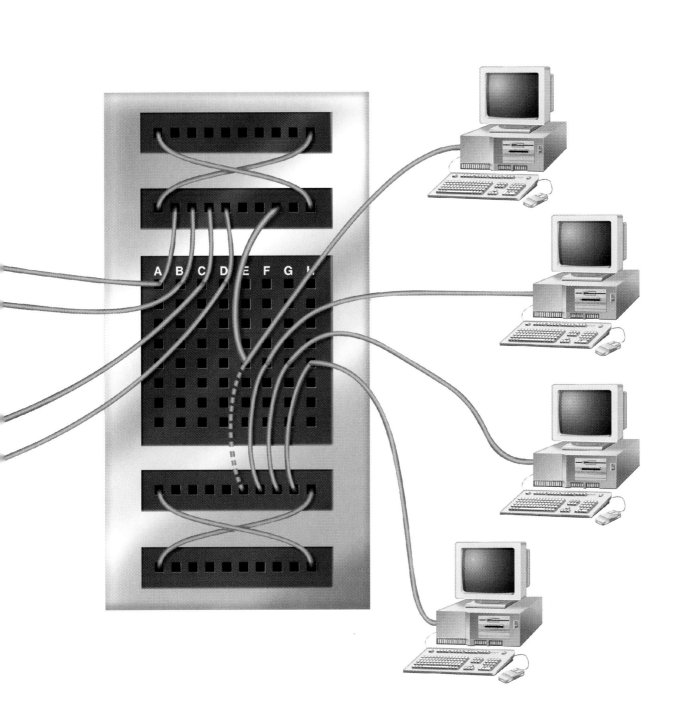

A *patch panel* is used to route network signals between wires in the walls and ceilings to network hubs and other network segments. A short cable, called a patch cord or *patch cable*, is used to interconnect the different circuits.

The *patch panel* is used to route wiring connections to the proper devices and network links. The workstations, hubs, and network links that belong to a larger network all come together at the patch panel. A patch cord is connected between devices that need to communicate. For example, a patch cord might be used to connect a workstation wiring run to a hub wiring run.

Wireless LANs

A network can be more than wires, software, and interface cards. A network can be wireless. A recent trend in networking technologies is to isolate the workstations from the network backbone. In doing so, a virtual network is created by a miniature radio transmitter and receivers. This allows laptop computers or computers in remote locations to be members of the network society, sharing data, information, and other LAN resources as if they were physically connected to the LAN.

Facts

Wireless LANs generally use high frequency radio signals to communicate between workstations and the central control unit. A central unit called a transceiver is connected to a hub port. This device translates the wireless protocol into a protocol understood by the hub. In essence, the transceiver is a network router or bridge (see Chapter 8, "Network-to-Network Connections," for details on bridges and routers). Information is received into the antenna of the transceiver and sent out over the LAN. The workstation has a card that connects to an antenna that sends network requests through the air to the transceiver. All information is relayed back and forth between the two transceivers as if they were physical network interfaces. The user, networking software, and the wired LAN doesn't know or care that a virtual wireless connection exists.

The disadvantages of a wireless LAN are its cost, as well as a potential security problem due to eavesdropping by others. Also, interference from sources such as lights and other radios can be a problem.

Cabling and Connections

Coaxial Cable

K eeping interference out and information in is important to any signal application, whether it is a television antenna drop, modem cable, printer cable, phone line, or computer network. Coaxial cable was designed to help with these two goals. During the 1950s, AT&T Bell Labs developed the first coaxial cable. This cable was designed with a center signal conductor and an outer shield that is usually at reference or ground potential. Such a cable prevents electrical interference from being generated, and prevents outside interference from sources such as motors, fluorescent lights, and computer timing circuits.

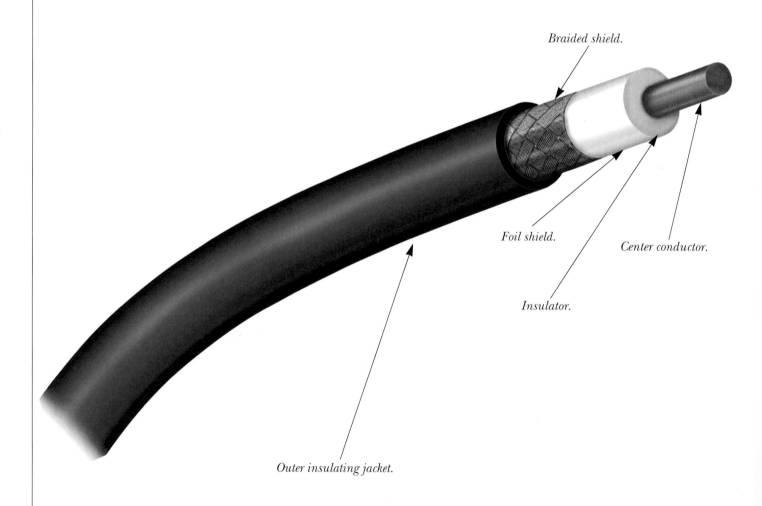

Braided shield.

Foil shield.

Center conductor.

Insulator.

Outer insulating jacket.

Facts

Coaxial cable is composed of an outer insulating jacket. The material used for this jacket is either PVC (polyvinyl chloride) or Teflon. PVC is used wherever cable runs aren't in an air plenum, such as in suspended ceilings or cold air returns. Teflon is used when cables are routed through air plenum spaces mainly because in fires PVC releases toxic fumes but Teflon does not.

The shield can be braided wire, foil, or both. The more demanding the application, the higher the shielding requirements. Under the shield is a plastic insulator which serves to insulate the center conductor from the shield. The center conductor is usually a solid copper wire, but some manufacturers produce a stranded center wire.

Solid wire tends to break and provides a poor connection, so it is used mostly in CATV applications.

Table 5.1 lists some common coaxial cable types and their usual applications. It is important that the correct cable type be used for a given application. As a general rule, you cannot mix cable types in an installation because the characteristic impedance of the cable will change, resulting in network failures. The impedance of a cable is based on the ability of the cable to carry a certain frequency signal. Impedance is the complex electrical resistance imposed by a circuit, and it is usually associated with electrical resistance and capacitive reluctance. Impedance only comes into play with changing state electrical signals such as Alternating Current. If the wrong impedance is used for an application, signal loss can result.

Table 5.1. Common Coaxial Cable Types

Cable Type	Impedance	Uses
RG- 8	50 Ω	10BASE5
RG-11	50 Ω	10BASE5
RG-58	50 Ω	10BASE2
RG-62	93 Ω	ARCnet
RG-75	75 Ω	Television

Coaxial Cable Connectors

Coaxial cable requires special devices to connect the wires to network devices. The most common type of connector used within computer networks is called a Bayone-Neill-Concelman (BNC) connector. This type of connector is used in 10BASE2 EtherNet installations and ARCnet installations. An assortment of adapters is available for use with BNC connectors. Some of the more common connectors used in networks are the T Connector, barrel connector, and terminator.

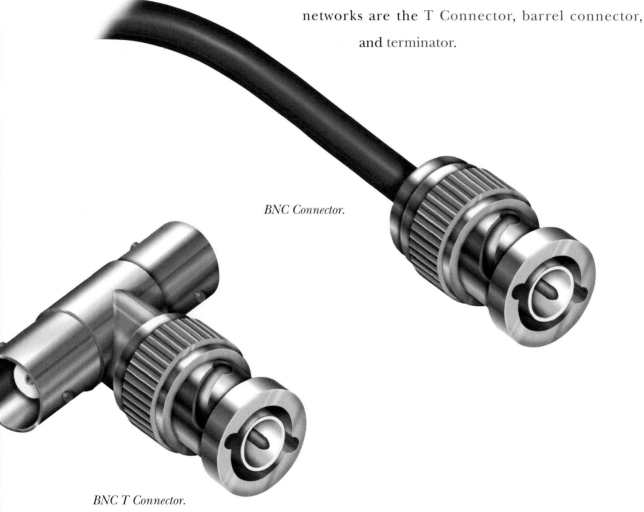

BNC Connector.

BNC T Connector.

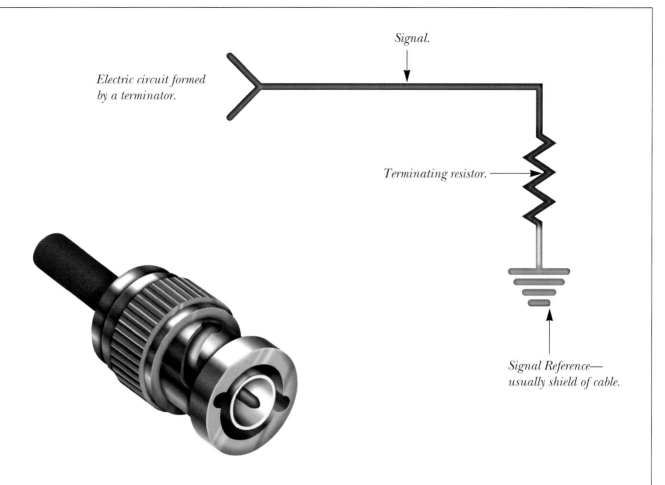

Electric circuit formed by a terminator.

Signal.

Terminating resistor.

Signal Reference— usually shield of cable.

BNC Terminator.

Facts

The connectors on the cable are the weakest point in any network. Most network problems can be traced to faulty cable connections. To avoid this, always use a good BNC connector. Resist the temptation to use a screw-on connector, and instead use a connector that crimps on the cable. Good crimping and wire stripping tools are required, but your initial investment in tools will pay off in properly attached connectors and reliable network operations.

A BNC T Connector is used in a 10BASE2 network configuration. This T is placed at all network interface cards, hubs, routers, and other network devices. Depending on the wiring configuration, a cable might be connected to form a bus network. At each end of any network cable, a terminator is placed to electrically terminate the cable.

A BNC terminator is a BNC connector with an added electrical component called a resistor. The resistor is soldered between the center conductor and the shield. For RG-8, RG-11, and RG-58 cable, a 50 Ω resistor is used. For RG-62 cable, a 93 Ω resistor is used.

Unshielded Twisted Pair Cable

U nshielded twisted pair (UTP) cable is a low-cost cabling method that is gaining in popularity. UTP is similar to telephone wire and is small and easy to install. ARCnet, EtherNet, and Token Ring use UTP without any problems. The only requirement is that the proper network interface card be selected to operate with UTP.

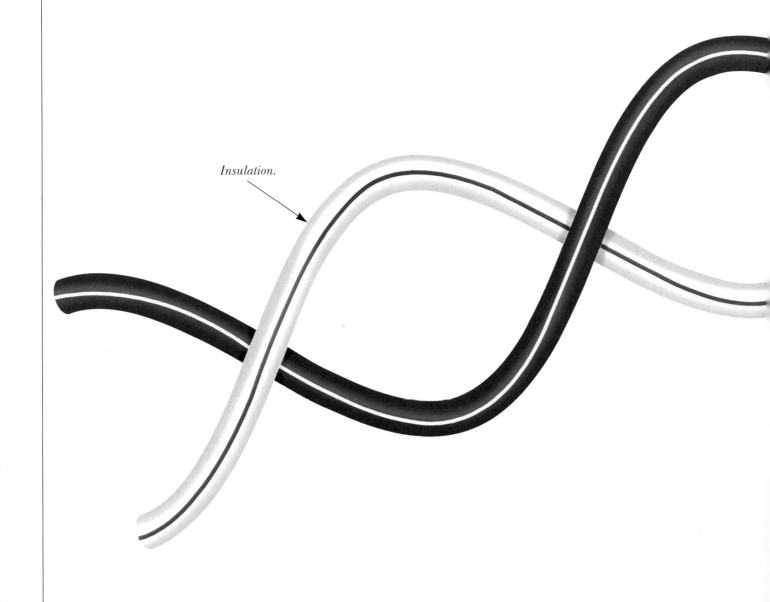

Insulation.

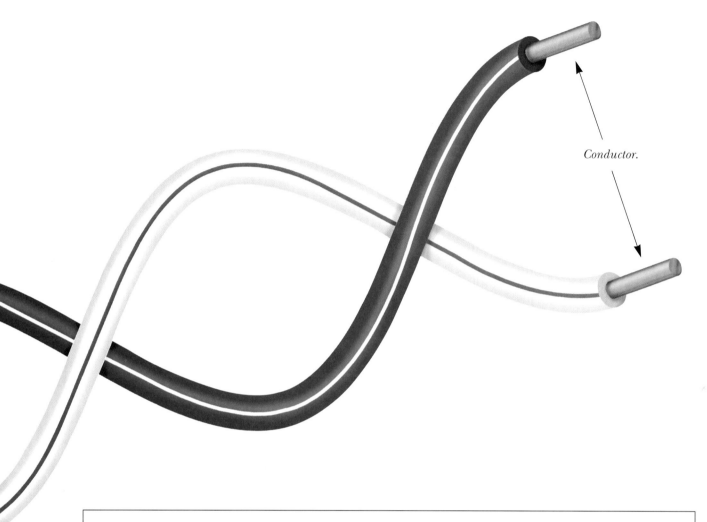

Conductor.

Facts

UTP is connected to network devices through a modular connector. Usually, this is an RJ-45 connector that contains room for eight wires. This type of connector is similar to the telephone connector used in your home, which is an RJ-11.

Table 5.2. UTP Wire Categories

Category	Application
1	Voice only; no data rating
2	Voice or data to 1Mbps
3	Voice or data to 10Mbps and 10BASET
4	Voice or data to 20Mbps, 10BASET, and Token Ring

UTP Connectors

UTP cable for networks is designed to transmit data reliably. Table 5.2 lists the different categories of UTP and their respective applications. The cable used in networks has an impedance of 100 Ω, and four pairs of copper wire of either 22 or 24 gauge. A typical EtherNet network would not use anything less than Category 3, but Category 4 or Category 5 would provide a more reliable installation with a minimal cost increase.

UTP, however, is different than the telephone cable installed in our homes and offices. The cable installed in homes is called quad because it contains four wires. These wires are not twisted, and they don't have any of the noise suppression that UTP has. Other types of telephone cable include a flat cable called silver satin, which generally is used to connect the phone set to the wall jack.

Signal Name	Wire Color	Pin Number
T2	White/Orange	1
R2	Orange/White	2
T3	White/Green	3
R1	Blue/White	4
T1	White/Blue	5
R3	Green/White	6
T4	White/Brown	7
R4	Brown/White	8

Facts

The RJ-45 connector is a plastic connector that is keyed. (A keyed connector is a connector with a plastic nib or a slot that allows the connector to be inserted only one way.) The connector is installed on the end of a cable with special crimping tools. RJ stands for registered jack. This means that the wiring in the jack follows a set standard; the most common is the ATT258A configuration. This standard indicates which color of wire and signal are applied to which pin within the connector. T represents tip, and R represents ring, conventions taken from the telephone industry. IEEE has a standard that is used in wiring 10BASET connectors, which is a subset of the ATT258A standard.

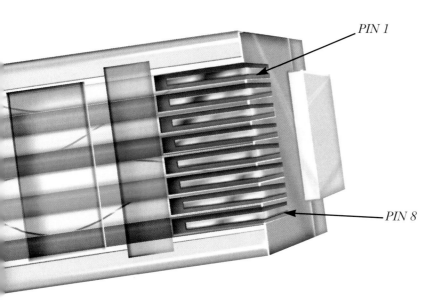

PIN 1

PIN 8

Signal Name	Wire Color	Pin Number
T2	White/Orange	1
R2	Orange/White	2
T3	White/Green	3
R1		4
T1		5
R3	Green/White	6
T4		7
R4		8

Fiber Optic Cable and Connectors

Fiber optic cable represents the latest in networking technologies. Fiber optic systems are great for carrying a huge amount of information at extremely high speeds. Pioneered by the telephone industry, fiber optic systems offer endless potential uses for data communication. Imagine a single cable that can carry computer data, video information, and telephone conversations. Fiber optic cable will soon bring this to reality. Some of the emerging standards for fiber optic transmissions are FDDI, 10BASEF, and FOIRL.

Facts

Fiber optic cable is great for applications requiring high data transmission speeds and immunity to electrical interference. Because fiber optic cable provides electrical isolation, concerns associated with different grounding potentials between buildings are eliminated, as are worries about damage from lightning or power line spikes.

The cable is constructed of a tough outer jacket, made of either PVC or Teflon (notice that the selection of outer jacket material is the same for coaxial cable). If the fiber optic cable will be placed in an air plenum, then Teflon-coated cables are needed.

Immediately inside the cable are Kevlar fibers, used to strengthen the cable. Kevlar is such a strong material, it is used in many bulletproof vests. Below the Kevlar layer is a plastic coating that cushions the fiber center. The center is called the core and is constructed of glass or plastic fibers. The size of the core varies but there are two standard sizes, 62.5 microns and 100 microns, with 62.5 microns being the most common. Between the core and the plastic coating is another layer called the cladding. This layer is used to reflect light back into the core.

The cable is connected at each end with a connector. The ST connector is used on most commercial applications; it has a locking feature similar to a BNC connector. To install a connector onto a fiber optic cable involves squaring the cable end, polishing the end to remove any scratches (because scratches tend to attenuate the signal), and gluing the cable to the connector. A curing oven is used with certain adhesives. After the connector is attached, the connection is solid until someone crushes it or the cable is cut. The cutting, polishing, and curing of the connector is done by the cable installer.

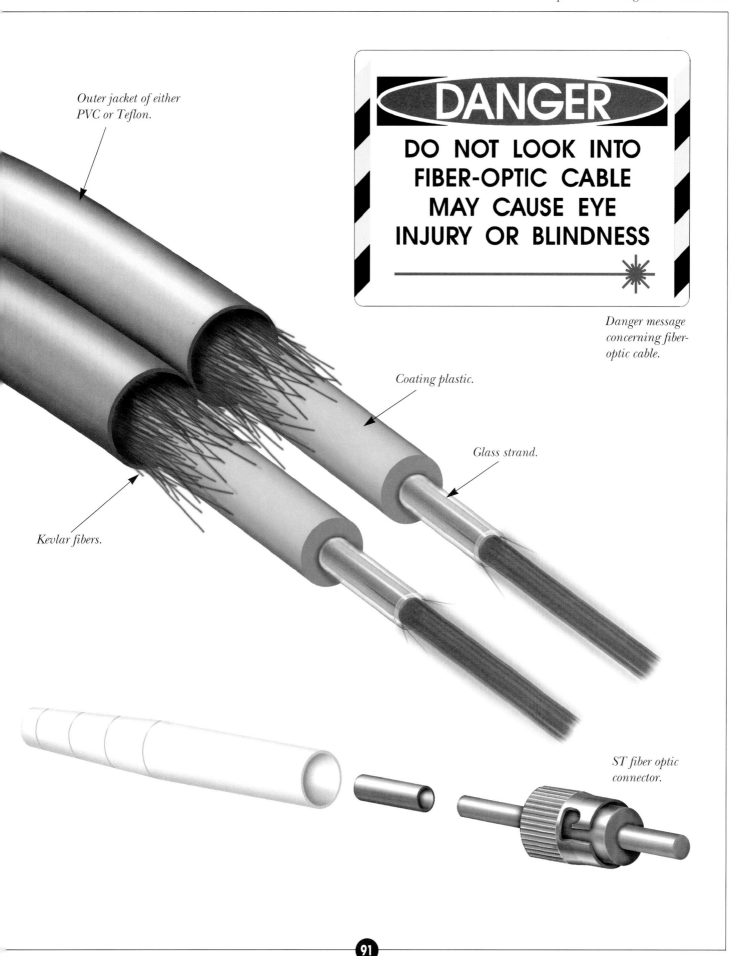

Outer jacket of either PVC or Teflon.

DANGER

DO NOT LOOK INTO FIBER-OPTIC CABLE MAY CAUSE EYE INJURY OR BLINDNESS

Danger message concerning fiber-optic cable.

Coating plastic.

Glass strand.

Kevlar fibers.

ST fiber optic connector.

Common Cabling Problems

Network failure can result from several problems. Some of the most common problems relate to the physical installation. These problems include network runs that are of excessive length, improperly terminated cables, bad connectors, and improper cable types. To avoid many of these problems, the installation should be planned and carried out by someone with adequate knowledge and experience.

Proper Ethernet Cable Connection.

EtherNet adapter card.   *BNC T connector.*   *Thin coaxial cable.*

Avoiding Connection Problems

- Connect a BNC T connector directly to the EtherNet device. Do not use a short cable (a pigtail) between the T connector and the device.

- Connect EtherNet cable to the T connector. If at the end of the circuit, use a 50 Ω Terminator.

- Use only crimp-on EtherNet connectors. The twist-on type of connector could cause network problems.

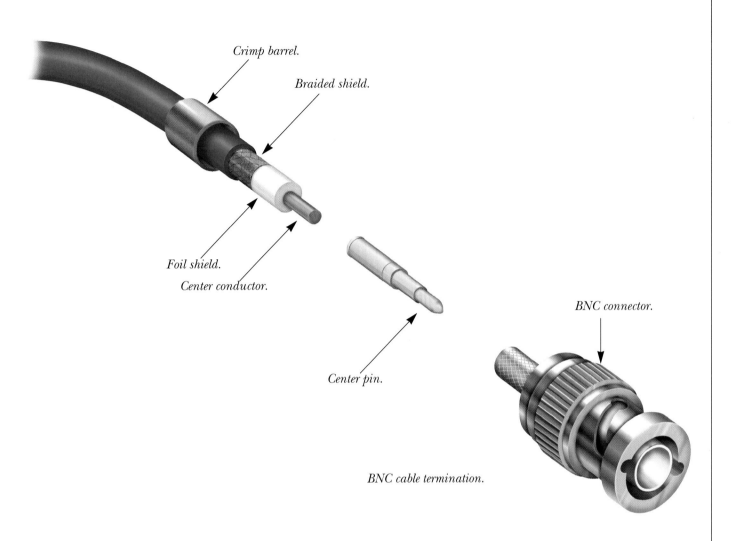

Crimp barrel.

Braided shield.

Foil shield.

Center conductor.

BNC connector.

Center pin.

BNC cable termination.

Proper BNC Connector Assembly

BNC termination is one of the most critical network connections in a 10BASE2 EtherNet or ARCnet network. To properly terminate the cable, a good quality cable stripper and crimping tool are needed. The illustration shows the components of a 10BASE2 EtherNet BNC connector assembly.

The BNC connector is comprised of a crimp barrel, center pin, and the actual connector. The cable is stripped to reveal the shields and center conductor. The center pin is slipped onto the center conductor. This pin is lightly crimped to the cable with the crimping tool. Then the cable is placed into the connector and the crimp barrel is moved over the shield and cable and crimped into place.

Network Interface Cards

After the cable is installed, a network interface card (NIC) must be placed into the computer. This card, along with some software, provides the necessary components to connect a workstation to a network. All network cards placed into IBM PC-compatible computers are similar. The only way to tell the difference might be through manufacturers' part numbers. Most cards provide a socket for an optional boot PROM (programmable read-only memory). This boot PROM sends out a message on the network that tells the server to download an operating system to the workstation.

This EtherNet adapter includes connections for three popular networking topologies. The RJ-45 connector is used to connect to 10BASET cabling; the BNC connector is used to connect to 10BASE2 cabling; and the AUI port is used to connect to a 10BASE5 network interface. The address for an EtherNet card is contained in a hardware PROM and cannot be changed. The only configuration usually associated with these cards is for memory, interrupt, and input/output port locations.

Boot PROM.

Configuration jumpers.

RJ-45 (10BASET).

AUI port.

EtherNet NIC.

16-bit bus.

IDE bus interface.

BNC (10BASE2).

ARCnet is usually associated with coaxial cable. This network card is typical of most ARCnet cards. It contains a 16-bit bus interface, BNC network connector, and locations for boot PROMs. The network address for each board is set by switches or jumpers. Some manufacturers make the switches accessible through the rear connector plate.

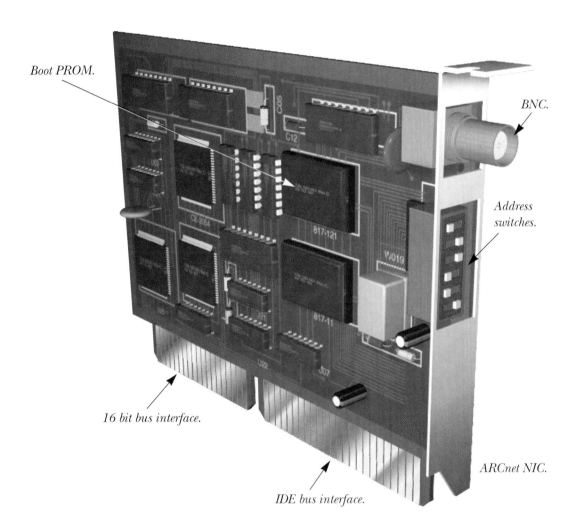

Boot PROM.

BNC.

Address switches.

16 bit bus interface.

ARCnet NIC.

IDE bus interface.

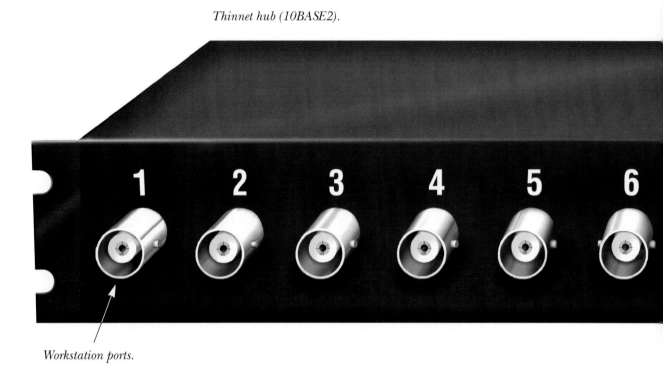

Thinnet hub (10BASE2).

Workstation ports.

Network Interconnection

In most networking technologies, some type of device is needed to interconnect network segments and workstations. Such a device is known by any of several names, including hub, media access unit (MAU), and concentrator. Some of these devices are passive and do not contain any electronic components that condition the network signals. Other devices are active and contain electronic components that strengthen the signal, remove unwanted noise, route traffic from one port to another, and filter network traffic.

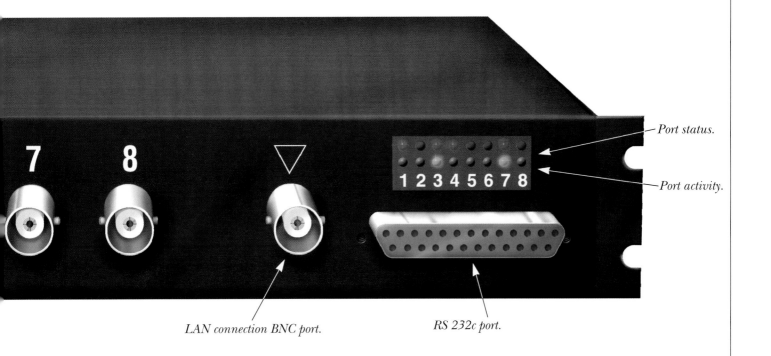

Port status.

Port activity.

LAN connection BNC port.

RS 232c port.

Facts

Allhubs consist of the same basic components: a place to connect the workstations or workstation LAN segments, a connection to other LAN hubs, and some status and activity lights called light emitting diodes (LEDs). These LEDs can show if a wire is improperly terminated or open, and also can show LAN activity along a network segment. Each workstation port is a BNC connector or an RJ-45 connector for EtherNet hubs, a BNC connector for ARCnet hubs, or an RJ-45 or IBM-type connector for Token Ring. Some hubs also include a 25-pin serial connector to connect an external ASCII terminal to aid in configuration and setup of the hub.

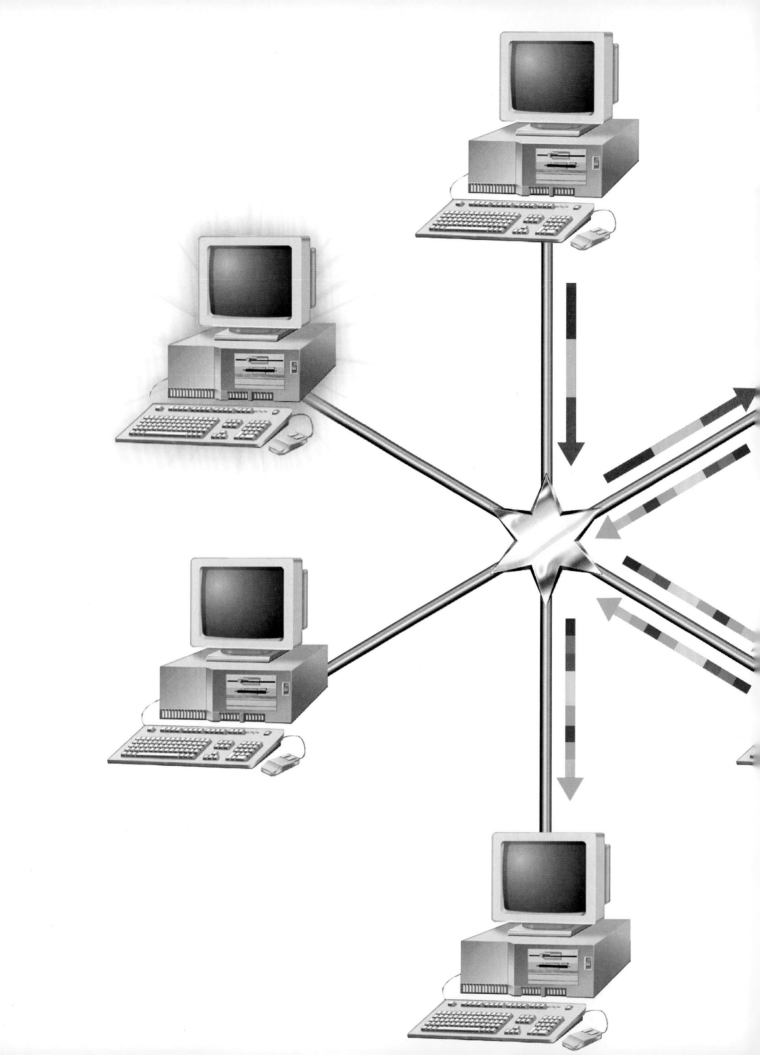

Communication Protocols

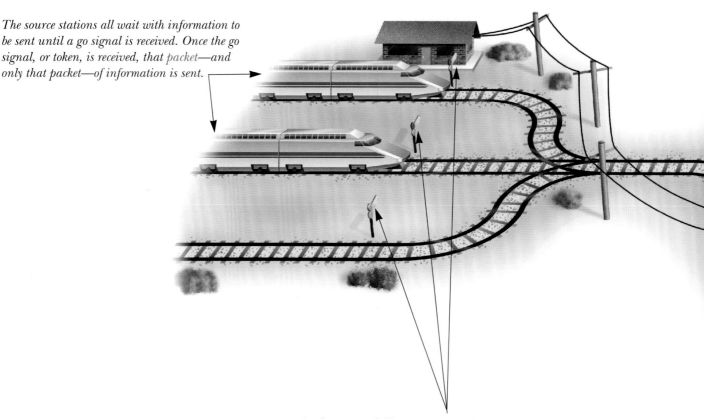

The source stations all wait with information to be sent until a go signal is received. Once the go signal, or token, is received, that packet—and only that packet—of information is sent.

A token is much like a train signal. It signals the sending station to allow a train to leave a station, in much the same way a token is sent to a node to allow the node to release its packet of information. Only one packet can be on the network at a time, just as only one train at a time is allowed out of a station.

Token-Based Networks

T oken-passing networks such as ARCnet and IBM Token Ring incorporate a signaling mechanism. This mechanism is used to control which stations on a network can send information and when they can do so. As in a train yard, only the node with the token (the "go" signal) can send information. The information is then allowed to travel to its destination. Once it arrives at the destination, an acknowledgment can be sent to the starting station.

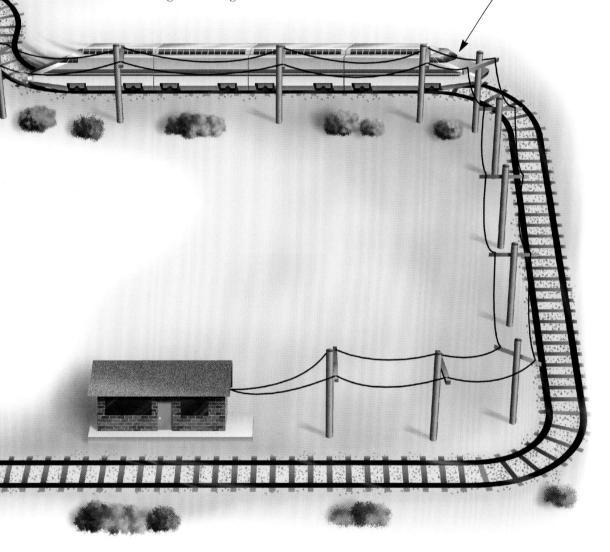

The destination station is where the information is received; all information is unloaded when a data packet arrives, just as a train's cargo is unloaded as soon as possible after the train's destination is reached.

The station that is receiving a train returns information that the train is welcome to arrive—and later, that it has arrived. On a network, similar acknowledgment messages are sent.

A data packet is much like a train. The preamble carries source and destination addresses just as the train engine—via the engineer—carries source and destination information. The data traveling on the network is the cargo in the cars. The error checking information which is sent following a data transmission is equivalent to the inventory records and travel logs stored in the train's caboose.

Facts

A packet of information on a token network is controlled and prioritized much like a train's schedule is controlled and prioritized. The tokens in a token network help to control and prioritize the message packets. Also, only a limited number of computer stations can be on a token network, as only a limited number of trains can be on a given track traveling between stations.

ARCnet Network

The ARCnet protocol is a simple architecture for small networks. It is a token-passing architecture. The token is passed from network node to network node. Any node that possesses the token is allowed to transmit data onto the network. After transmission, the node releases the token to the next node. All packets are acknowledged when they're received, and permission is granted to forward information as needed. All ARCnet frames use a header field, called the alert field, which is filled with six 1s.

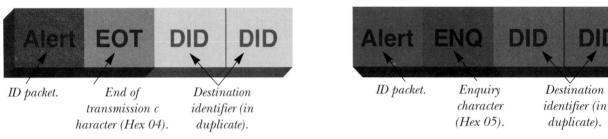

ID packet. End of transmission c haracter (Hex 04). Destination identifier (in duplicate).

ID packet. Enquiry character (Hex 05). Destination identifier (in duplicate).

The ITT (invitation to transmit) frame is the network token. The node that possesses this frame is allowed to send information onto the network. In order to transmit data, the FBE (free buffer enquiry) packet is broadcast by this node. The ITT frame begins with an EOT (end of transmission) character (ASCII code 04). Following EOT are two bytes, each containing the destination identifier (DID). This destination address is duplicated for error checking.

The Free Buffer Enquiry (FBE) is used to determine if the destination node can accept a data frame. Contained in the

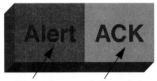

ID packet. Acknowledge character (Hex 06).

The ACK and NAK frames are used for handshaking. The ACK packet is used to acknowledge an FBE request. ACK is a positive response and tells the requesting node that it is okay to send a data frame.

If the destination cannot accept a data frame, it sends a negative acknowledgment (NAK) to the node that sent the FBE. When a NAK is sent, the data frame will not be sent.

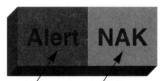

ID packet. Negative acknowledge character (Hex 15).

Cyclic Redundancy Check.

Start of header.

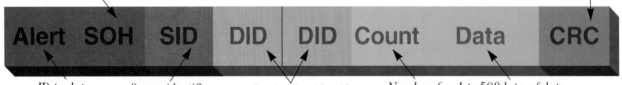

ID packet. Source identifier. Destination identifier (in duplicate). Number of data items. 1 to 508 bytes of data.

The PAC frame is the actual data being sent on the network. The PAC frame begins with a start of header (SOH), and then contains the source address, destination address (in duplicate), a count field indicating the number of data bytes to be sent, the data bytes themselves, and finally a CRC for error checking of the packet.

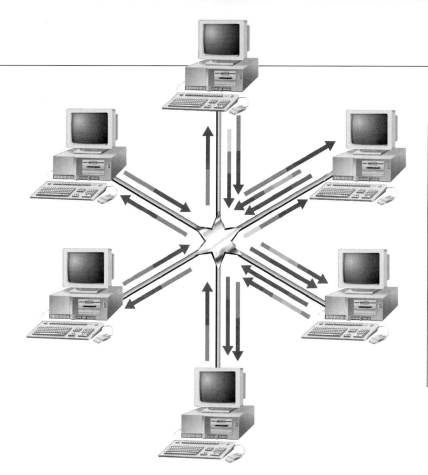

Facts

An exchange of information in the form of handshaking is used on an ARCnet network between the sending and receiving stations. The exchange is initiated by an FBE packet being sent to the receiving station. That packet is then acknowledged, data is sent in a PAC packet, and receipt is acknowledged by an ACK packet. This exchange occurs until all data has been sent.

Once the sending station has sent all its information, the token is released to another station.

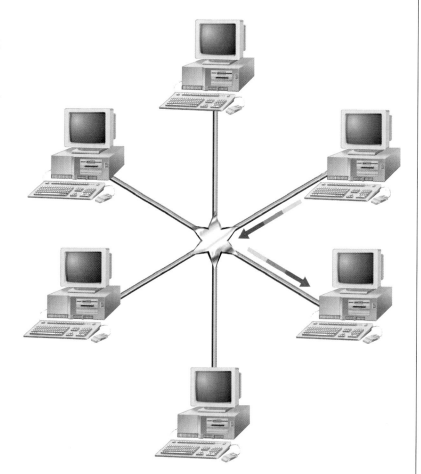

ARCnet is such a reliable protocol that it is used in factories, where noise from motors, welders, and other devices generates electromagnetic interference. ARCnet's reliability stems from features such as built-in error checking in the form of a cyclic redundancy check (CRC) and data redundancy in the form of a duplicated destination station address. The duplicated destination station address helps to guarantee reliable data delivery of the packet. This is useful in a harsh environment where interference could cause a disruption of information on the network.

Token Ring

IBM's Token Ring network is based on the IEEE 802.5 token network model. Each ring is limited to 260 workstations on twisted pair wire. The token is generated as soon as a transmitting station is finished sending a frame. Unlike under ARCnet, redundancy of destination addresses is not included. The specified physical topology for a Token Ring network is a star.

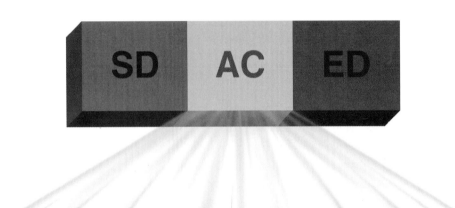

P,R = Priority bits.
T = Token.
M = Monitor.

The token is three bytes long. Packet priorities are set in the AC field. If the T field is set to 1, the packet is only a token; otherwise, the packet contains data.

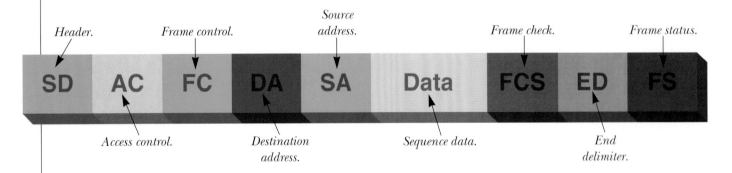

The Data/Command frame contains the data that is being sent from the source to the destination node. Information relating to source and destination addresses is contained within the frame.

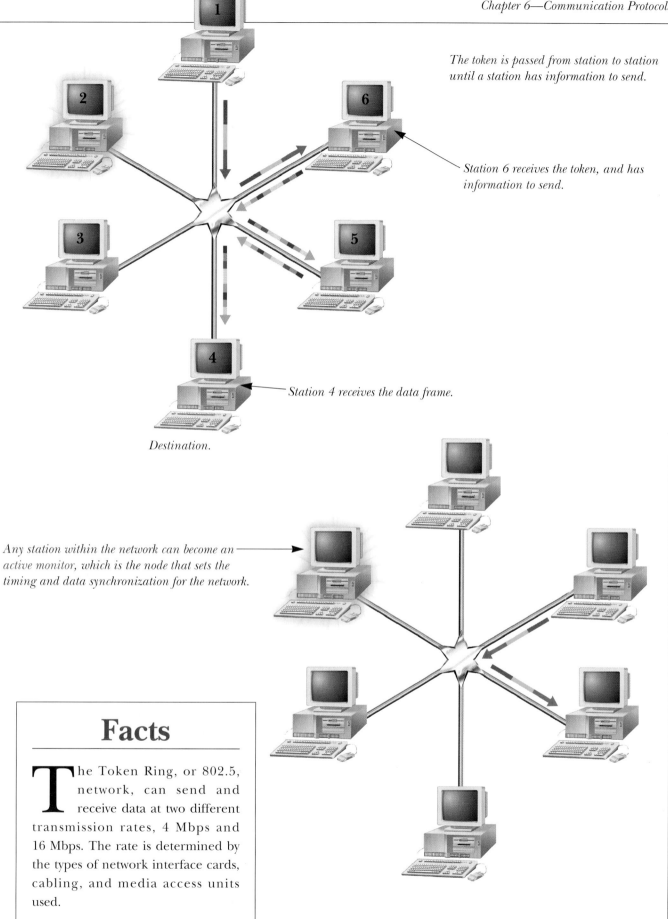

The token is passed from station to station until a station has information to send.

Station 6 receives the token, and has information to send.

Station 4 receives the data frame.

Destination.

Any station within the network can become an active monitor, which is the node that sets the timing and data synchronization for the network.

Facts

The Token Ring, or 802.5, network, can send and receive data at two different transmission rates, 4 Mbps and 16 Mbps. The rate is determined by the types of network interface cards, cabling, and media access units used.

FDDI

Fiber Distributed Data Interface (FDDI) is another token-passing network topology. FDDI is another of the IEEE 802.5 token networks. The topology consists of two physical rings. One ring moves data in a clockwise motion; the other ring moves data in a counterclockwise motion. Each ring can include over 1,000 workstations.

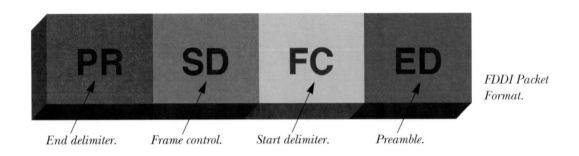

FDDI Packet Format.

End delimiter. Frame control. Start delimiter. Preamble.

Frame status.   Frame check.   Source address.   End delimiter.   Start delimiter.

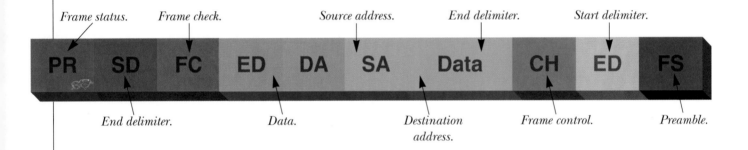

End delimiter.   Data.   Destination address.   Frame control.   Preamble.

Facts

FDDI is a good topology to use for high-speed applications, including network backbones and high-end computing applications. Some applications that will need the performance of FDDI in the future—or that use it already—are multimedia, video conferencing, and imaging.

There is a variant of FDDI called CDDI (Copper Distributed Data Interface). This is a specification that allows both shielded and unshielded twisted pair cable to share the same communication protocols associated with FDDI.

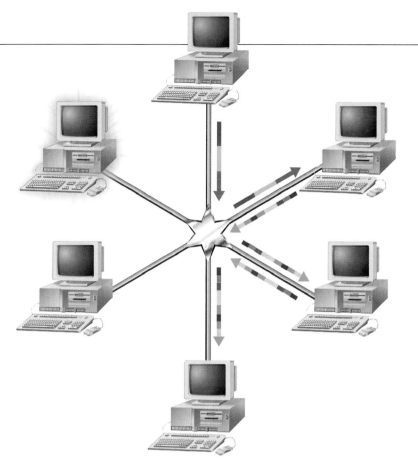

All FDDI packets start out with a preamble, much
the same as Token Ring packets do. Next, there is
a start delimiter, used to synchronize data. When
the network is not moving data, a preamble idle
pattern is constantly sent. The idle symbol has a
bit pattern of 11111. A minimum of 16 five-bit
idle symbols separates frames.

The frame control determines the addressing of the
frame. The address may be either 16 or 48 bits in
length and include the type of frame, as well as
whether the frame is data or command.

The data field contains a variable number of data
items that are being sent from the source address to
the destination address. These data fields may be
as short as 1 byte or as long as 4500 bytes.

The frame check packet is a CRC packet. This
packet is responsible for providing information to
determine if the data has arrived intact. It is
examined at the destination node and compared
with the value computed for the arriving packet. If
the two agree, the data is considered to have
arrived reliably.

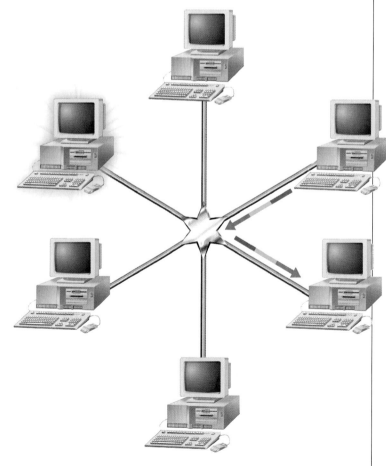

EtherNet

The EtherNet network protocol is the most widely used networking methodology today. Because EtherNet does not use a token to control data transmission, several data packets can be on the network wire at once, heading to several different destinations. The network does not set priority for data elements. Data is sent and received on a first-come, first-served basis.

Facts

EtherNet, IEEE 802.2, and IEEE 802.3 make up the EtherNet protocol family. These three protocols are all inter-related, but software must be configured properly to handle the appropriate data packets. All the packets include a cyclic redundancy check that is used to guarantee data reliability—this data-checking algorithm is so powerful that corrupted data packets usually can be reconstructed.

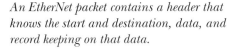

An EtherNet packet contains a header that knows the start and destination, data, and record keeping on that data.

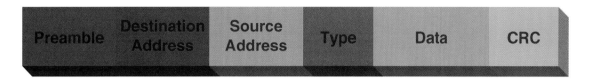

Preamble	Destination Address	Source Address	Type	Data	CRC

These data packets contain some handshaking information at the front, and then source and destination addresses. These are the addresses of the sending and receiving stations.

A significant difference occurs in the next two fields. EtherNet uses a type field to indicate the type of application for which the data was being formatted. IEEE 802.3 uses this as a count of data bytes in the data field. This difference makes the two packets mutually exclusive. The sending and receiving stations must be set up correctly for the particular type of EtherNet being used.

Preamble	Start of Frame Delimiter	Destination Address	Source Address	Length	Data	CRC

101010...0.   *10101011.*   *Length of data.*   *Data within frame.*   *Cyclic redundancy check.*

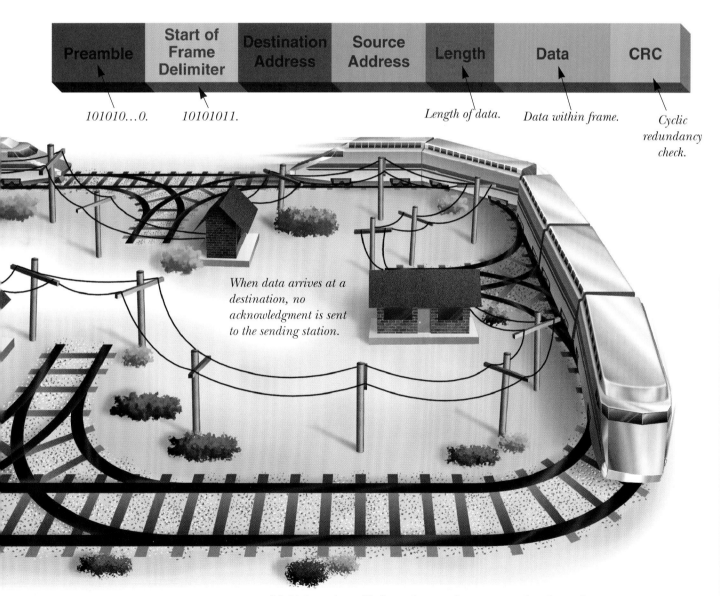

When data arrives at a destination, no acknowledgment is sent to the sending station.

Multiple packets of information may be present on the wire at the same time. Since each packet knows where it came from and where it is going, this is not a problem unless collision occurs.

SPX/IPX

SPX and IPX data packets are native to Novell's NetWare, which is a family of networking software. NetWare provides for file sharing and print sharing to workstations. Also included are client-server capabilities through remote procedure calls and the SPX/IPX programming interface. The client/server capabilities allow an application to be located on the file server and to have client applications running on the workstations. This allows a division of responsibility between applications.

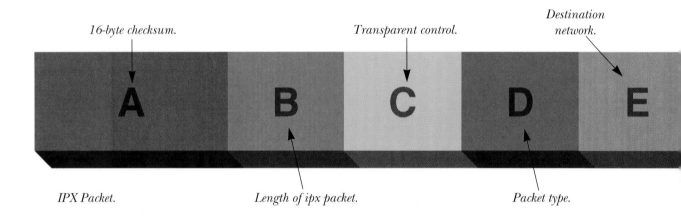

16-byte checksum.   Transparent control.   Destination network.

IPX Packet.   Length of ipx packet.   Packet type.

Internetwork Packet eXchange (IPX) is the heart of the NetWare protocol suite. This is a connectionless (messages are sent without expecting a response) protocol that provides routing and addressing capabilities. The routing information is based on a protocol developed for TCP/IP (discussed later in this chapter) networks called RIP (Routing Information Protocol). This allows information to be sent to workstations that are not on the same physical network.

Sequenced Packet eXchange (SPX) is a bidirectional communication protocol. This type of protocol exchanges information between two systems and expects a response to each message sent. This is known as connection-oriented communications. The remote procedure call (RPC) protocol is used in remote printing and Remote Console Management.

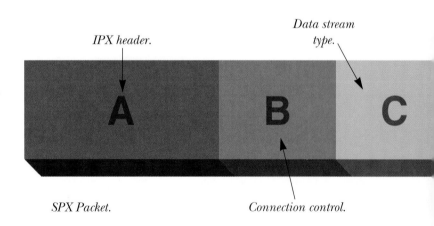

IPX header.   Data stream type.

SPX Packet.   Connection control.

Facts

IPX and SPX are closely related, but not identical in function (SPX is more of a transport protocol while IPX is both a network and transport protocol). They provide the basis for applications to communicate on a peer-to-peer basis without any interaction from the file server. Since IPX is a connectionless protocol, it is faster; however, there is no guarantee of delivery. SPX, on the other hand, is connection-oriented and verifies that data not only has been delivered, but delivered in the correct order. Together, IPX and SPX provide a complete communication suite for NetWare networks and applications.

The difference between IPX and SPX is in the verification of packets sent and received. IPX just sends them and does not really care if they have been delivered properly while SPX is concerned with accurate delivery.

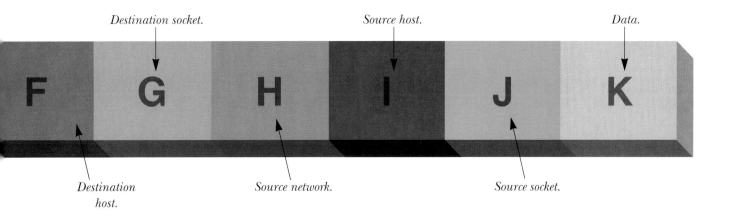

Destination socket.   *Source host.*   *Data.*

Destination host.   *Source network.*   *Source socket.*

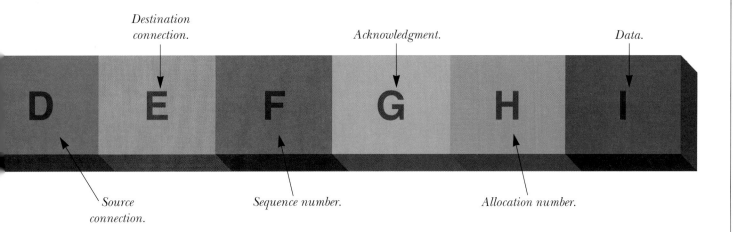

Destination connection.   *Acknowledgment.*   *Data.*

Source connection.   *Sequence number.*   *Allocation number.*

TCP/IP

The TCP/IP protocol stack is the basis of the internetworking protocols. Internet Protocol (IP) is responsible for connectionless communication. It delivers messages between systems but does not guarantee delivery or receipt of the messages. Transmission Control Protocol (TCP) is a connection-oriented protocol responsible for reliable delivery of messages. Together, they form the core of the internetwork protocol suite.

Facts

The usage of TCP/IP and related protocols has increased in the last few years. TCP/IP is the basis for the public Internet. Other functions of TCP/IP are remote procedure calls, SNMP, and Telnet.

Remote procedure calls are a mechanism of communication between programs running on different systems. A remote procedure call is a protocol that allows applications to call and execute routines on a remote computer. These routines return information and variables to the calling procedure. Simple Network Management Protocol (SNMP) is used to manage network devices, collect diagnostic information, and control network device configuration. Telnet is a method of remote terminal connection and emulation.

TCP/IP is a collection of different but related protocols, and continues to change and be redefined almost daily.

Network File System (NFS) is a method of using remote disk and file systems on a local computer. NFS is an upper-level protocol that provides the mechanism to transfer information between a workstation and a remote file server. The remote disks appear to be physically attached to the local computer.

IP Protocol Packet.

TCP/IP Protocol Stack.

The protocol packet for TCP is composed of many 32-bit packets. The header packet is at least six 32-bit packets long. The protocol fields contain information about source and destination ports. A port is like a remote program. These programs communicate information through the network by passing data packets. Next are a sequence number, an acknowledge number, some flags that contain information relating to the disposition and type of information that is being sent, a checksum, and finally the data.

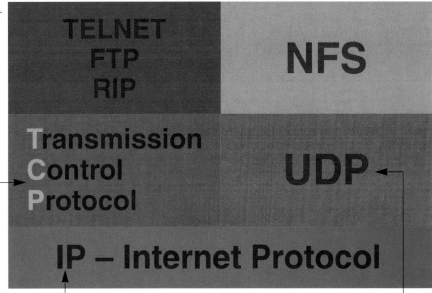

IP is a connectionless protocol responsible for communication between systems and for moving data between systems. The protocol packet contains a header packet and data. The header has six or more 32-bit records. Each of the records contains information relating to addressing, type of application being serviced, size of data being sent, and checksum information.

User Datagram Protocol (UDP) is not connection-oriented, but provides the basis for remote file systems and management protocols. It is a more efficient protocol than TCP because it doesn't have the overhead associated with a connection-oriented protocol. UDP receives information from IP and passes it on to upper-level protocols such as NFS .

Network Line.

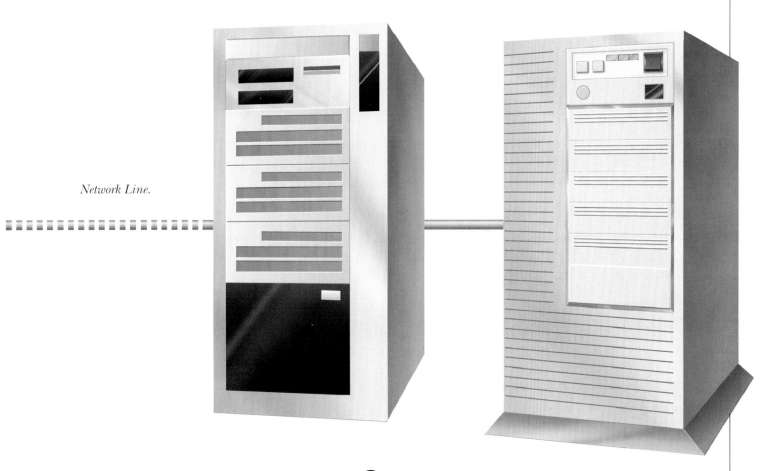

Network Pipes

The communication of computers through networks is not limited to files and disk services. Other services need to be provided. These services allow programs running on two different computers to communicate in a transparent, standardized format. One way to allow this to happen is through network pipes.

Facts

Pipes form an interface into the network that allows the programmer to control applications that need to share information. In much the same way that a single train can enter a tunnel on one side of a hill and exit on the other side, a pipe directs information from the output of one program or process into the input of another program or process. On a network this output program is usually on a client computer and the input on a server. The pipe interface is well-defined and has allowed a whole collection of software to be developed. The pipe mechanism allows workstations, servers, minicomputers, and mainframes to exchange information. This exchange of information remains transparent to the computer users.

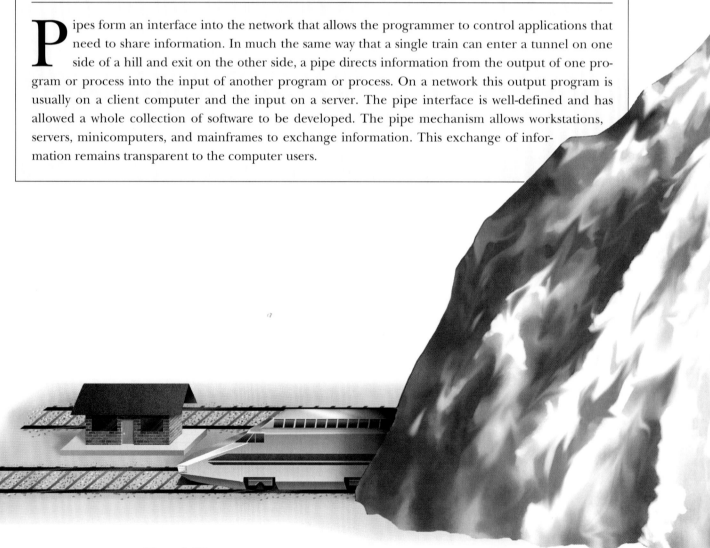

Network Pipes.

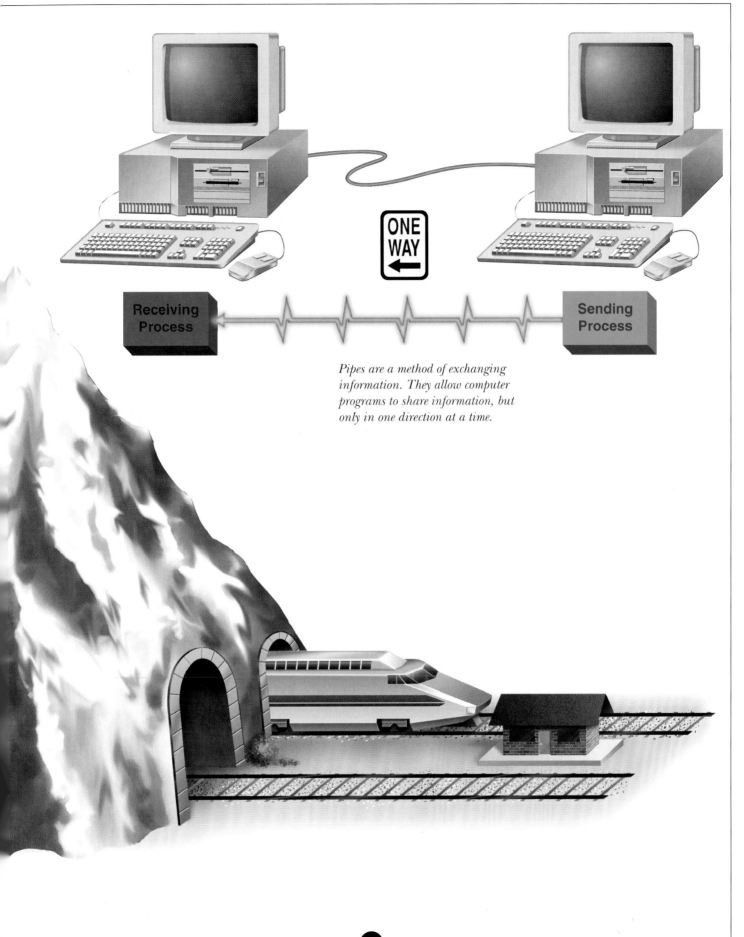

Receiving Process

Sending Process

ONE WAY

Pipes are a method of exchanging information. They allow computer programs to share information, but only in one direction at a time.

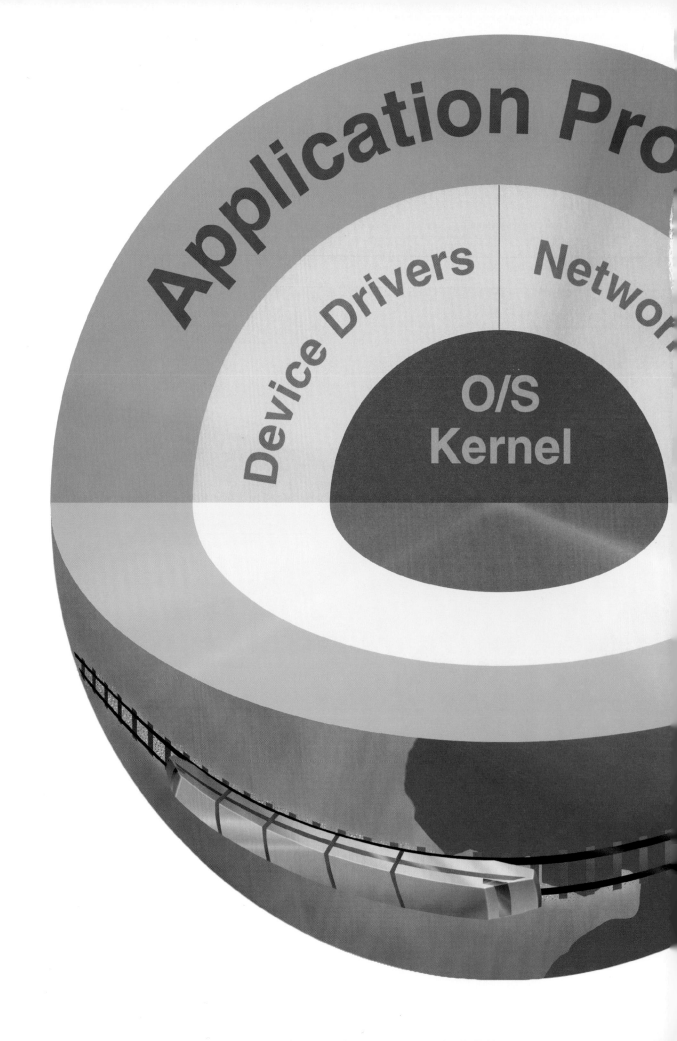

Operating Systems

How a Network Operating System Works

Network operating systems (NOS) have been in use since the late 1970s. A NOS is an operating system that can do multiple things at once. This is referred to as multitasking. The multitasking is optimized to schedule resources such as disks and networks.

Some of the early NOS were iNDX from Intel and Sharenet from Novell. These early systems were the beginning of NOS. All of the current NOS are derived from these products.

The NIC device drivers translate kernel requests into the proper hardware requests to send information to and receive information from the network.

The NOS kernel contains all of the low-level operating system functions. These functions include process communication methods, device driver requests, scheduling requests, lock controls, and error checking.

Many different types of application programs can run on a network server (depending on physical memory). Some programs collect statistical information on the file server's performance, some programs analyze error conditions, and other programs provide services for databases and electronic mail.

System Scheduler

NIC Device Driver

Operating System Kernel

Physical LAN

Server Application Programs

The system scheduler is responsible for overall system timing. This is the part of the NOS that decides when disk requests are going to be serviced, when print jobs are going to be printed, when network requests will get responses, and which local server application programs should run. The scheduler is in constant communication with the NOS kernel (core operating functions).

As a request for a file comes in from the NIC, it is passed to the scheduler. The scheduler then sets up the request and notifies the disk device driver that a file is needed. The disk device driver gets the file and informs the kernel, which in turn sends the requested information out to the NIC driver and across that LAN. The same sequence of events is used for print jobs. Local applications may or may not follow the same sequence—this is determined by the application programmer. But all requests for services still must go through the kernel.

The disk device driver is responsible for turning disk access requests into commands that disk controllers can understand. The disk controller is the device that translates software commands into physical access for information on a disk drive.

Disk Device Driver

Printer Device Driver

Some device drivers are printer-aware. They have the necessary intelligence to process printer codes before the codes are sent to the printer. Other printer device drivers do not contain the intelligence for printer codes and, thus, the codes are passed directly to the printer, and the printer must translate them.

Network Operating System.

Single-User Operating Systems

A single-user operating system is like the disk operating system (DOS) found on most personal computers. This type of operating system can only perform one task at a time and cannot be used effectively to offer devices for network sharing without additional software components.

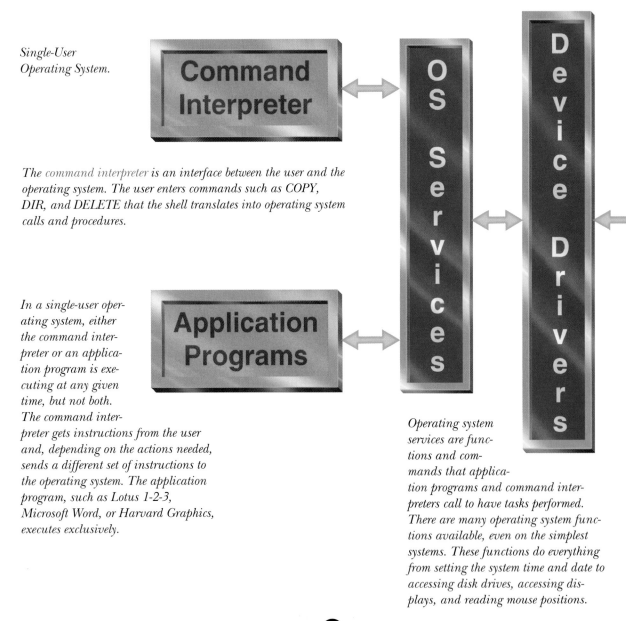

*Single-User
Operating System.*

The *command interpreter* is an interface between the user and the operating system. The user enters commands such as COPY, DIR, and DELETE that the shell translates into operating system calls and procedures.

In a single-user operating system, either the command interpreter or an application program is executing at any given time, but not both. The command interpreter gets instructions from the user and, depending on the actions needed, sends a different set of instructions to the operating system. The application program, such as Lotus 1-2-3, Microsoft Word, or Harvard Graphics, executes exclusively.

Operating system services are functions and commands that application programs and command interpreters call to have tasks performed. There are many operating system functions available, even on the simplest systems. These functions do everything from setting the system time and date to accessing disk drives, accessing displays, and reading mouse positions.

Facts

There are many operating systems available for computers. At one time, only large computers, called mainframes, could perform multiple tasks. These tasks divided the mainframe into many little computers that individual users could use. When personal computers (PCs) started to appear in the mid-1970s, a method of interacting with the user was needed. This was when the single-user, single-tasking operating system first appeared.

Today, the computer world is changing again, and on people's desktops are PCs with operating systems capable of supporting many tasks and sometimes many users. This multitasking started because desktop computers became so powerful and so underutilized. At one time a mainframe did not have the power of even a now almost archaic 286 PC. With the proper operating system, a PC can service several users, but more importantly, a single user can do many tasks at once. That was not possible way back when mainframes roamed the offices.

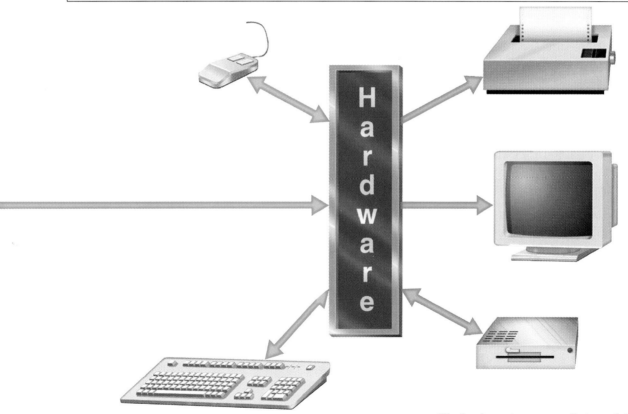

Device drivers are used to translate operating system functions into hardware commands. These commands tell disk drives which read head and cylinder to use to read the information on a disk. Device drivers also are responsible for commands that satisfy a user request for the color blue or the letter A to be displayed on-screen. Device drivers handle the hardware commands to send a print job to the printer, and even handle the commands to interface to a network.

The hardware is not actually part of the operating system, but is controlled by operating system controls. The operating system sends output to a display screen and printer, sends and receives information from disk drives and network adapter cards, and receives information from the keyboard and mouse.

Comparison of Single-User Operating Systems and NOS

I n single-user operating systems, only one function can be performed at a time. Multitasking operating systems and network operating systems are capable of performing many tasks at once. A single-user operating system could be used as a file server, but then only one workstation could be serviced at a time, since each request from a workstation is a single task. Because this would be inefficient utilization of hardware and network resources, network operating systems are designed to perform many tasks at once, and must handle many requests from different sources.

Single-User OS.

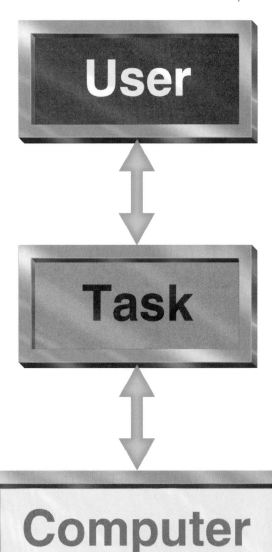

A single task at a time can be performed using an operating system like MS-DOS. The task completely consumes all available processor time as well as all available memory. In a multitasking operating system, each application is allowed the maximum amount of memory that can be consumed, but the less memory an application uses, the more that is available for other tasks.

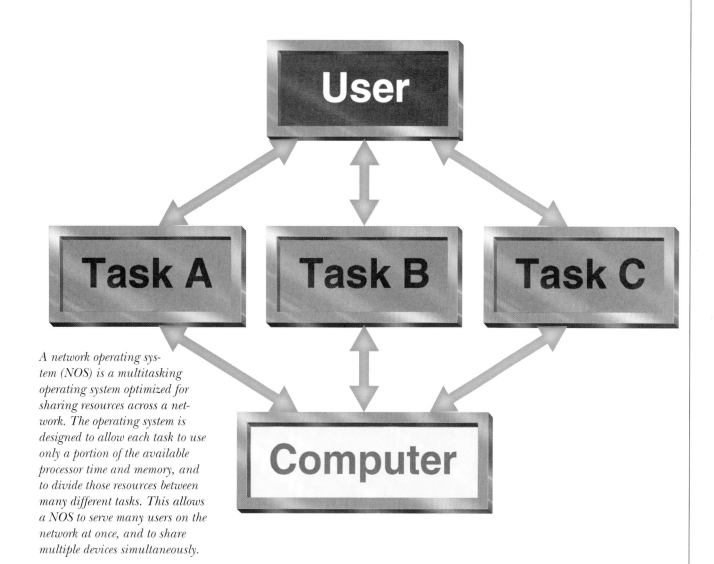

A network operating system (NOS) is a multitasking operating system optimized for sharing resources across a network. The operating system is designed to allow each task to use only a portion of the available processor time and memory, and to divide those resources between many different tasks. This allows a NOS to serve many users on the network at once, and to share multiple devices simultaneously.

Facts

Network operating systems are very good at their given task: Dividing up resources and sharing them between many users. However, all this functionality brings complexity. The many parts of a NOS must be carefully administered in order for user requests to be handled properly. If the NOS doesn't have enough resources to share among users, it may not even function in a standalone mode.

While single-tasking operating systems could run on older-technology computers without much memory or processing power, a NOS needs lots of memory and processing capability. Novell NetWare 3.1, for example, needs a 386 PC with at least 8M of RAM while DOS needs only an 8088 and 512K of RAM. In addition to these hardware requirements, a NOS usually requires someone with plenty of training and experience to set it up and keep it running.

Access Control

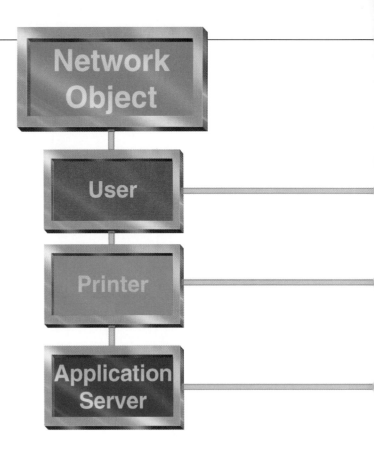

Once a NOS is set up and running, and all the shared resources are available, access to these resources must be controlled. Most users immediately associate access control with user names and passwords, but it includes much more than this. Access control encompasses the control of network objects including users, printers, disks, and applications, as well as the properties associated with each object.

All this information is stored in a structure on the file server. This structure is the *access control database* that the NOS uses to control, manage, and share resources between users.

Facts

Typically, everything on a network is controlled by the network operating system. The users, printers, disk space, and applications are all controllable objects. Each of these objects has certain properties that need to be controlled. Some properties are shared by many objects while others remain unique to a certain object. This control of objects helps to allocate resources fairly to many users, and provides security to sensitive data and applications.

User objects usually are associated with a particular computer and network user. Properties associated with a user are passwords, login times, object membership, and so on. Some of these properties help to make the network a secure environment for data and information, because in essence they are the keys to the network. These properties determine who can access the server, when the server can be accessed, and what on the server can be accessed. Other types of user properties provide information such as the user's real name.

Applications and devices also have properties. These properties not only control access, but may be used to control how the object operates. One example is the type of printer forms used by a printer. A printer property may be used to reference a form number that corresponds to a blank payroll check, an engineering change order form, or a shipping insert. These items help the flow of information and resources and allow many different users access to a small number of devices.

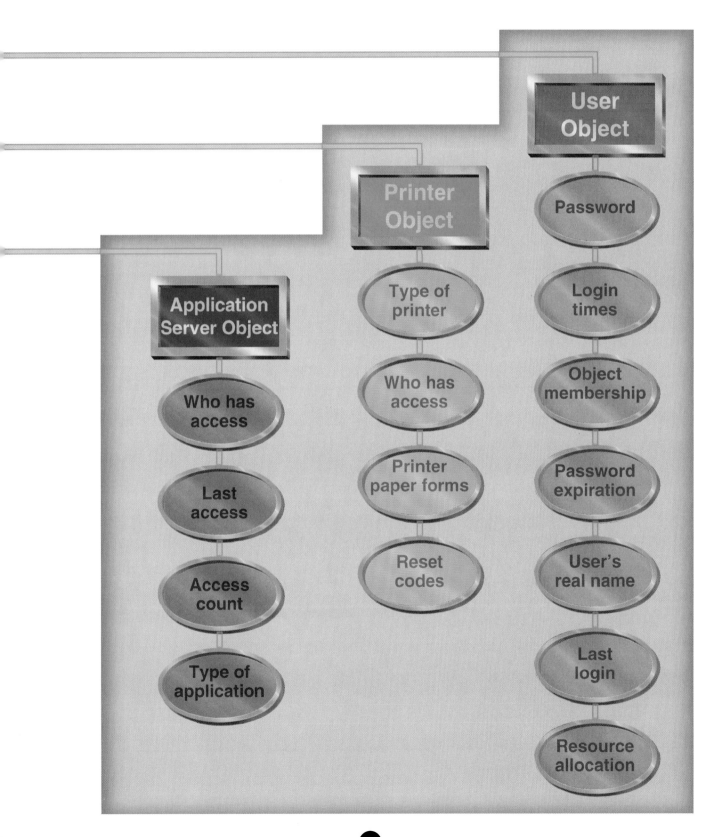

Examples of properties tracked in an access control database.

Directory Services

A new concept of managing users and information in a server is emerging. The resources and users are members of a hierarchical data structure called a *tree*. This structure contains information about different file servers, users, applications, printers, print queues, and shared information.

When all the individual departments and divisions decide to interconnect their networks, you get a more complex tree. This tree has many branches in common with the simple network, but all these branches come together to form a larger tree. The larger tree is made up of each department and each department's file servers, users, and printers.

Root

ACME_NET

Accounting

Engineering

CAD

Marketing

Facts

As networking technology changes and becomes more complex, newer management and organization methods must emerge. These methodologies are integrated into the newer NOS. Only time and hard work will tell what the future has in store for NOS. Many organizations have introduced a single four- or five-user network and had it blossom into a 1,000- or 10,000-user network. As these networks grow, it helps to have a method of adding descendants and assimilating them into the whole family. This allows for more efficient flow of information within the organization.

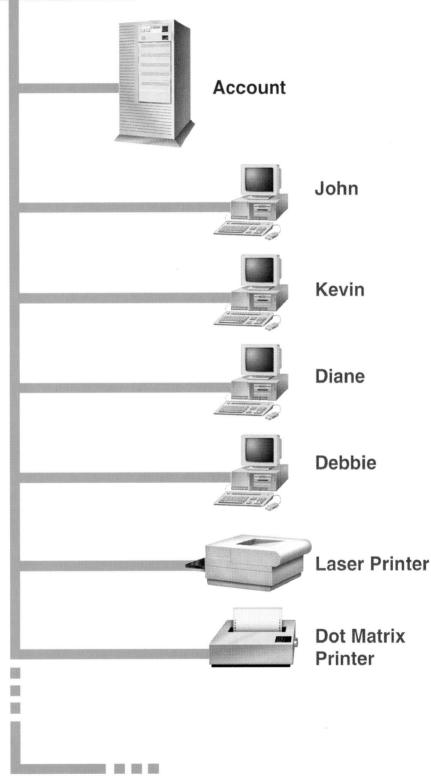

A simple network has a root and many descendants, just as a family starts from a single set of parents and then grows to include a child and then siblings, and a grandchild and then siblings, and a great-grandchild and then siblings, and... well, you get the picture. The children of a simple network would be the file server, users, and print devices. Each of these items relates to the parent in its own manner. In an organization, a department such as Accounting or a division such as Widget Manufacturing might serve as a parent to users, network devices, and so on.

Directory Services.

Peer-to-Peer LANs

Information sharing is becoming more and more important as more people share computers and information technology. With all the interest generated by networks, a simple and inexpensive approach to networking was introduced for small networks (two to five users). This simple method of networking is called *peer-to-peer*. This allows devices and resources on one PC to be shared with devices and resources on another PC. Person A can copy or access a report on Person B's hard drive, Person B can print out Person A's report on his own laser printer, and Person A can send the final copy of the report to the company president using Person B's fax/modem. This type of sharing can help control cost and resources within small organizations.

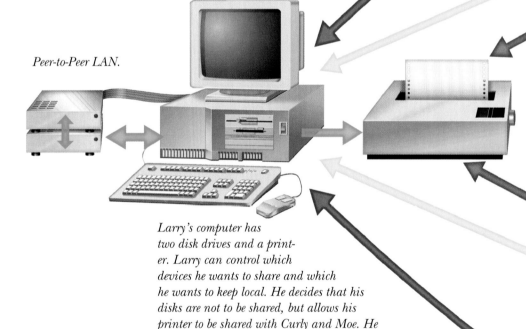

Peer-to-Peer LAN.

Larry's computer has two disk drives and a printer. Larry can control which devices he wants to share and which he wants to keep local. He decides that his disks are not to be shared, but allows his printer to be shared with Curly and Moe. He also needs access to Curly's hard disk, but only for reading information. This is called read access. However, he needs both read access and write access to Moe's hard drive.

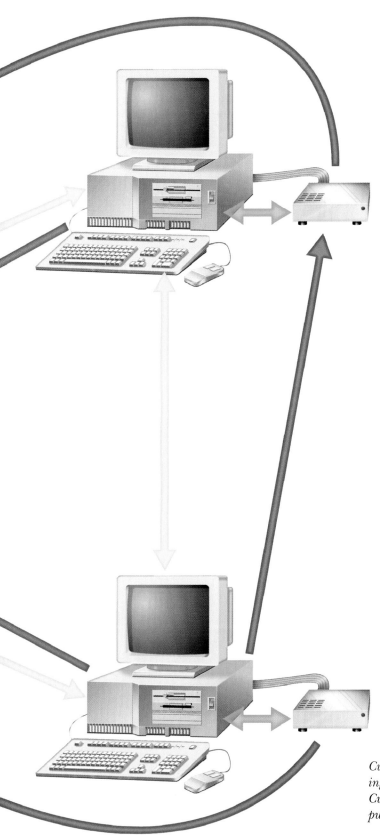

Facts

Peer-to-peer LANs are a method of sharing information between users. Software loaded on each single-user system adds some functionality of the NOS, allowing a user on another computer to request and share information. Information that does not reside on a user's workstation is referred to as residing on a remote workstation. The remote computer serves information to users at their own workstations. In a peer-to-peer network, the remote computer may at the same time request information from the user's local workstation.

The user's local workstation will serve the information to any requesting workstation. In essence, a single-user computer is turned into a file server. The network tasks run as terminate-and-stay-resident (TSR) tasks on each workstation, and are triggered to life through a hardware mechanism called an *interrupt.*

An interrupt is an external event that causes software to be executed. The NIC listens for information being sent on the network that is addressed to its address. When there is inbound information, the NIC triggers a hardware interrupt, which pauses the computer and the current task being run by the user of the workstation, and processes the network request. After the network request is handled, the local user's task resumes execution. On a larger computer the interrupt would be acknowledged and scheduled by a scheduler for execution.

This is how a single-tasking computer can handle network requests without using a scheduler. This type of activity is only appropriate on small networks where there is limited traffic and information exchange. If it occurred on a regular basis, the user of the workstation might not be able to use the local computer due to network activity.

Curly only lets Larry use his hard drive and then only for reading. Curly can write to Moe's hard drive whenever needed. Since Curly doesn't have a local printer, he uses the one on Larry's computer as a remote printer.

Server-Based LAN.

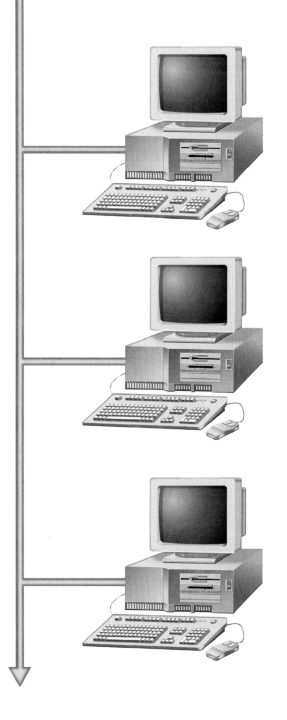

Server-Based LANs

Server-based networks have one or more file servers within the network. These file servers may have multiple disk drives, tape drives, and printers available. They also may be connected to more than one network at a time. All resources are available to users through the central file server.

The workstations in a LAN can access the devices offered by the file server. These devices appear on the local computer as local devices. Access to file server resources is usually controlled via login identification methods such as user names and passwords.

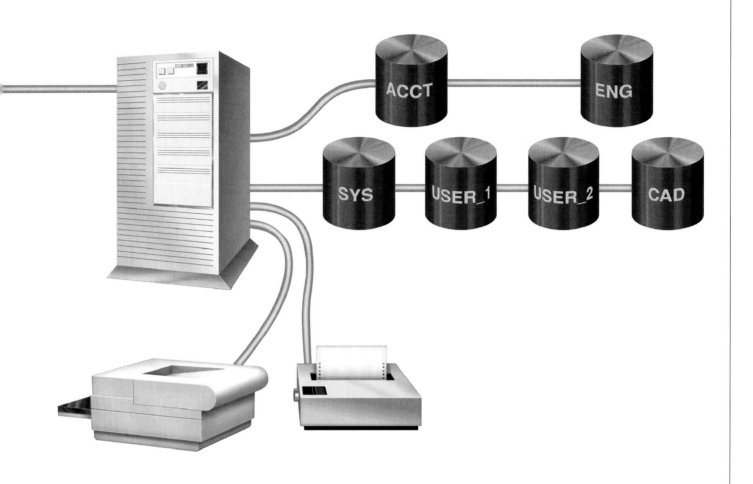

Facts

A file server is usually a powerful computer. It is not uncommon for file servers to have high performance central processing units, large memory systems, and fast input and output channels. A file server might contain more than 16M of physical memory, which is used to store the NOS, system buffers, and cache.

A cache is a special way of storing information that needs to be accessed quickly. A disk drive is a slow device, so cache memory would be used to store directory tables to speed up data access. Also, when a disk is read, more information from the disk is read into cache memory than was requested. Since many requests for information are followed by subsequent requests for the next information in sequence, this sort of caching allows disk information to be accessed more quickly than if the information were processed simply on a request-by-request basis.

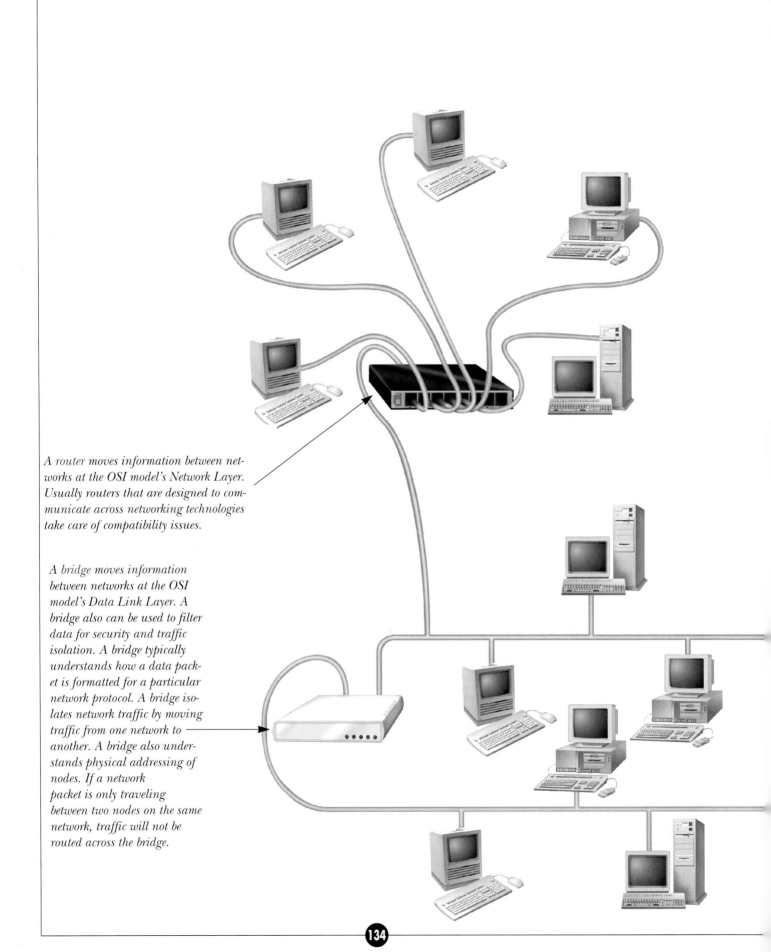

A *router* moves information between networks at the OSI model's Network Layer. Usually routers that are designed to communicate across networking technologies take care of compatibility issues.

A *bridge* moves information between networks at the OSI model's Data Link Layer. A bridge also can be used to filter data for security and traffic isolation. A bridge typically understands how a data packet is formatted for a particular network protocol. A bridge isolates network traffic by moving traffic from one network to another. A bridge also understands physical addressing of nodes. If a network packet is only traveling between two nodes on the same network, traffic will not be routed across the bridge.

Basics of Network Components

Computer networks are like the Energizer bunny: They keep growing, and growing, and growing, and… well, you get the picture. It isn't long before a network in one department needs to share some information that exists on another network in a different department. Whenever this happens, special components are needed to *interconnect* these networks.

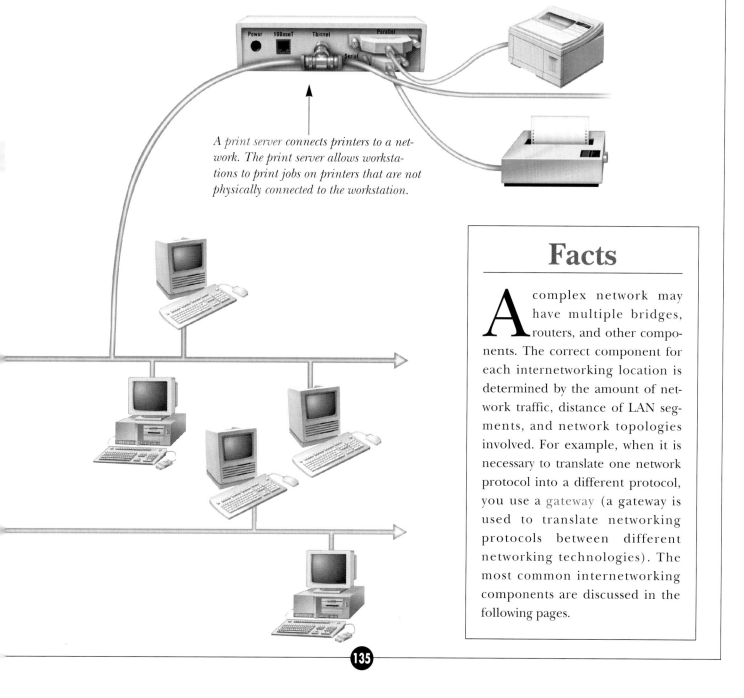

A *print server connects printers to a network. The print server allows workstations to print jobs on printers that are not physically connected to the workstation.*

Facts

A complex network may have multiple bridges, routers, and other components. The correct component for each internetworking location is determined by the amount of network traffic, distance of LAN segments, and network topologies involved. For example, when it is necessary to translate one network protocol into a different protocol, you use a gateway (a gateway is used to translate networking protocols between different networking technologies). The most common internetworking components are discussed in the following pages.

Routers

A network router is used to translate information from one network to another. The information is exchanged using logical address information. Although a router has access to physical information, only logical information is exchanged.

Routers also are little computers. Routers execute a special computer program that decides the best route for information to travel. Among the information considered are line cost parameters. Line cost is a value usually assigned by a network manager on a physical internetworking connection. A slower link generally has a higher cost, and makes for a more expensive (in actual dollars) route. The router's ability to evaluate cost helps it to funnel information down the most desirable network path. If there is only one path to the intended destination, then cost obviously isn't a factor.

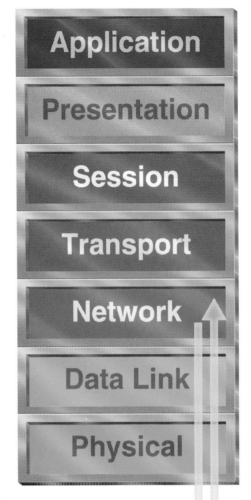

Where do IP addresses come from?
The IP address is allocated by a network information center in Virginia. A block of numbers is obtained by a network administrator. The network administrator then assigns each address to a single workstation and device at workstation setup time.

Facts

A router functions on the Network Layer of the OSI model and works with logical addressing. Because of this, information can be routed from one networking topology to another. A router can be used, for example, to tie together a Token Ring network and an EtherNet network. The physical address on the Token Ring network would be used on the Token Ring, and physical addresses would be used on the EtherNet. Individual workstations, however, would be referenced using their logical addresses.

A physical address is the address of an EtherNet card or some other hardware card. The logical address is a software address assigned by either a network manager or a program. An example of a logical address is the IP address.

Physical addresses are used on a network to communicate between devices. Two EtherNet devices have an addressing scheme different from two Token Ring devices. A router can take care of these addressing problems by using a higher-level addressing scheme. For example, a router will strip off the EtherNet physical address and add the Token Ring physical address. The information is tracked through the software or logical address.

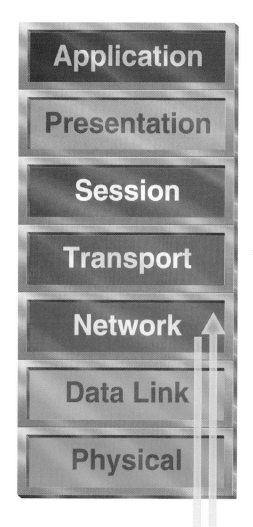

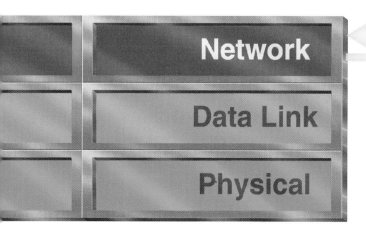

A router functions at the Network Layer of the OSI model. This is the layer of the OSI model where network node numbers are assigned to devices. For example, an IP address of 192.23.45.67 might be referenced at this layer, and information would be routed to it using logical addressing and referencing.

Bridges

As opposed to a router, a bridge works on the Data Link and Physical Layers of the OSI model. A bridge doesn't care what network protocols are in use—it only tries to transfer packets between networks.

A trend among networking manufacturers is to build brouters. A brouter is a combination of a bridge and a router (discussed in the preceding section, "Routers"). Most brouters have programs that run a set of routing instructions for a specific network layer protocol, yet still can move packets between networks of unsupported protocols.

Unsupported or unknown protocols are protocols the brouter does not have information on. Because it does not know any special methods of handling this information, the brouter passes the information through without modification.

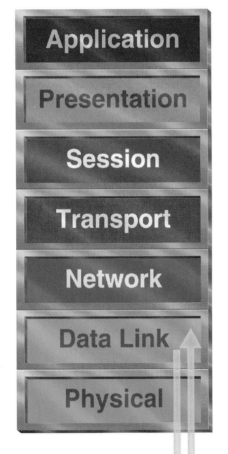

Facts

With a bridge, information is exchanged between nodes using physical addresses. Since a bridge doesn't have the overhead associated with a router, a higher level of performance is possible. A bridge usually is used to divide a large network into smaller areas of automation. This allows for heavily loaded networks to reduce their traffic load and thus increase performance.

The overhead on a router is due to the logical address translations. This occurs at a higher level of the OSI model, so the router must contend with more information. Because the bridge only works with physical addresses, it is faster at moving data packets, but is not usually usedto move information between different networking technologies.

A bridge looks at all source and destination addresses, then compares these addresses to an internal table of addresses. If the destination address for a given packet exists on another portion of the network, the packet is moved; otherwise, the packet doesn't cross the bridge.

Some bridges use a computer algorithm called a spanning-tree algorithm to determine when nodes are added to or removed from a network. This algorithm is used in a transparent bridge. A transparent bridge learns about all thenet-work devices at installation. This helps reduce setup time. A source-routing bridge is programmed at installation with node addresses of all current network components. As new nodes are added or removed, reprogramming is necessary.

Application

Presentation

Session

Transport

Network

Data Link

Physical

ink

cal

A bridge is used to move information between two or more networks. Information is translated at the Data Link and Physical layers.

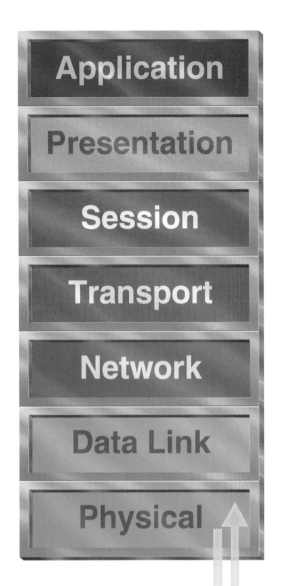

Repeaters

Of all the devices used to interconnect networks, the network repeater is the fastest and simplest. It is used to extend the physical lengths of LANs, and doesn't contain any routing intelligence.

A repeater is used when two network segments are approaching their maximum physical length, which is usually controlled by cabling limits.

A repeater functions at the Physical Layer of the network. As a packet is received, the data is broken into its most basic forms. These basic elements are then reconstructed into a new data packet and sent to the next network segment.

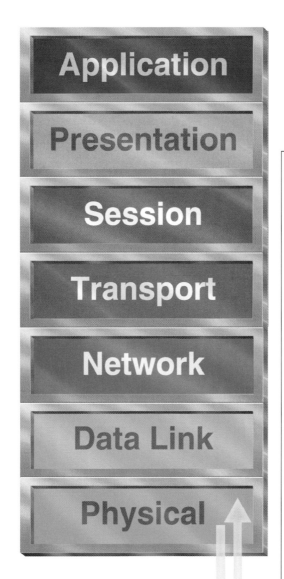

Facts

Since a repeater does not recognize hardware, logical and physical address information is retransmitted regardless of workstation location on a LAN segment. In all practicality, both LAN segments become one. Repeaters cannot be used to reduce traffic, as a bridge can, or to control traffic flow between networks, as a router can.

Any number of repeaters can be used on a network. It is a good idea to limit the number of repeaters on a LAN though there is no hard numerical limit. Use repeaters when needed, but don't overuse them. You pay a penalty in network responsiveness as more and more repeaters are added. In a small network (under 100 nodes), you would not usually need a repeater; however, a large network of several hundred nodes may have several repeaters. It depends how far the cables must run and how important it is for information to reach the remote nodes.

Because repeaters don't reduce traffic, an extended LAN can be built that contains a tremendous amount of traffic. If performance (throughput, bandwidth usage, response time) is your main concern in interconnecting networks, then bridges, not repeaters, are your best choice because bridges help to segment the network traffic.

Gateways

Agateway, also known as a protocol converter, is used to interface dissimilar networking protocols. Gateways are used in a variety of applications where computers from different manufacturers and technologies must communicate.

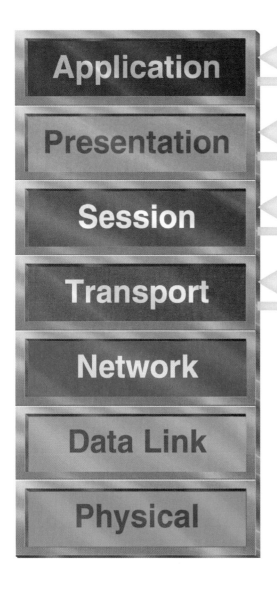

Gateway

Gateways are used to exchange information at the Transport, Session, Presentation, and Application Layers of the OSI model. The gateways know nothing about the Network, Data Link, or Physical Layers of a network.

Facts

The information that passes through gateways is peer-to-peer information that comes from applications, user interfaces, and end-user programs. Because each side of the gateway knows about the underlying networking technology of that part of the network, information can be received, rebundled, translated, and sent out the other side to the other network. Gateways are often used to interface between IBM SNA (System Network Architecture) and either EtherNet or Token Ring.

Gateways are slow and awkward devices. They are only used in extremely tricky cases such as connecting networks between SNA and EtherNet. Neither side of the network takes a performance hit, but exchange between the two networks is slow. These devices are not generally used on networks requiring high-speed information exchange.

Data switch.

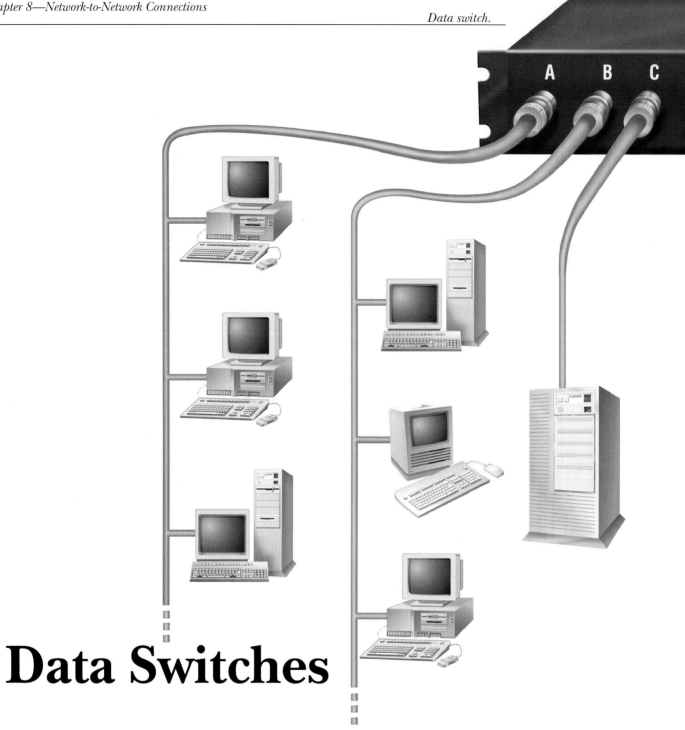

Data Switches

Data switches, or network switches, are used to provide a dedicated high-speed link between LAN segments. These switches generally are used in applications where traffic from one set of workstations needs to reach a single server.

Data switches usually analyze traffic and make a connection between devices needing to exchange information. It is a good way to set up mini-networks that also need to be interconnected. Consider three separate networks. Each network has a file server and some workstations. These workstations only communicate to a dedicated file server. Now suppose a single workstation needs information

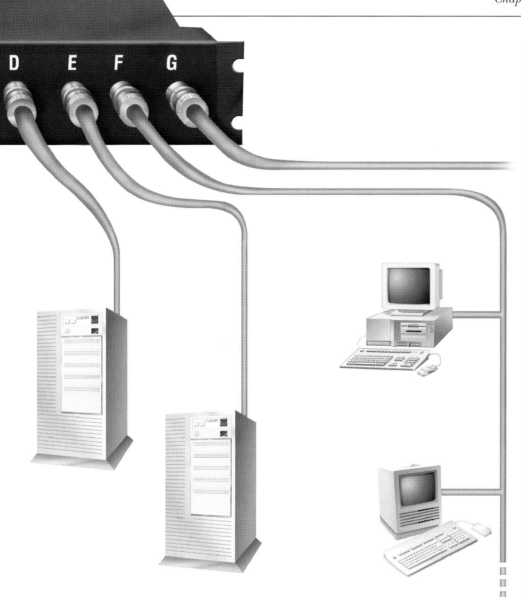

Facts

Network switches work at the Data Link and Network layers of networks. No modification of network information is performed by the switch. The switch only monitors network addresses to know if inbound traffic is bound for some other LAN segment. If so, an automatic switch connects the two appropriate LANs.

Data switches generally are used to connect networks that access and share data between the same set of file servers and workstations. These switches are not very efficient at switching multiple segments at high speeds. It has become generally acceptable to use switches when two networks need to occasionally share information. Some newer switches are capable of high-speed switch rates and can have performance exceeding that of a bridge, but usage of these is not widespread.

from another network's file server. The network manager could (a) physically connect both networks, (b) bridge both networks, or (c) use a switch. A switch allows each network to function as an independent standalone network. When a workstation needs to connect to a file server on another line, a connection between the two networks is made. After the communication is complete, the connection is broken. This also could be used to provide a hot backup to a file server. By switching the servers on and off of network segments, a hot swap could occur.

Print Servers

O ne thing a network does well is to share resources. To be shared, a device is usually connected to a workstation or to the file server. If, however, other servers and mainframes need to access the shared device, then a network device to facilitate device sharing is needed. If the device to be shared is a printer or plotter, you use a print server.

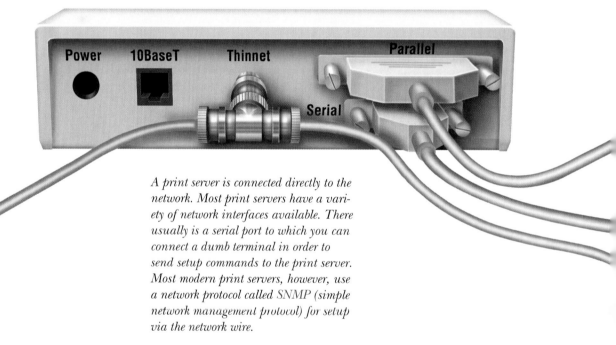

A print server is connected directly to the network. Most print servers have a variety of network interfaces available. There usually is a serial port to which you can connect a dumb terminal in order to send setup commands to the print server. Most modern print servers, however, use a network protocol called SNMP (simple network management protocol) for setup via the network wire.

A print server may have only one connection for a printer, but most have as a minimum both a serial and a parallel port to which you can connect devices. On some print servers, you can use each of these ports to connect several devices.

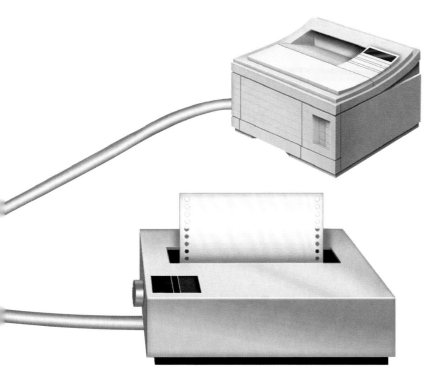

Facts

Print servers may communicate with many different hosts using different networking protocols. It is not uncommon for a print server to understand both TCP/IP and IPX. This allows the print server to print jobs from both a Novell NetWare server and a UNIX workstation. The print server handshakes with the print queue on the respective host and then accepts its job for printing. Jobs usually are accepted on a first come, first served basis unless the print server is configured specifically to prioritize print jobs.

A dumb terminal is an ASCII terminal that accepts information from the keyboard and sends it out over a serial port. It also receives information from the serial port and sends it to the display. There are no local processing capabilities.

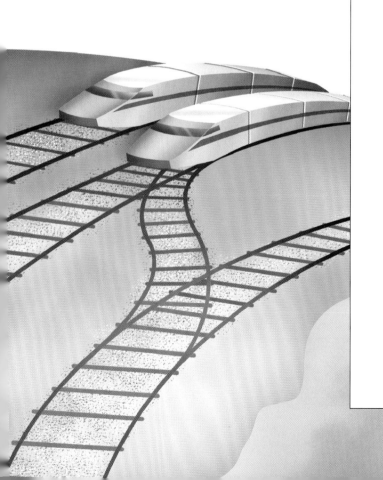

CHAPTER

9

MANs and WANs

Metropolitan Area Networks

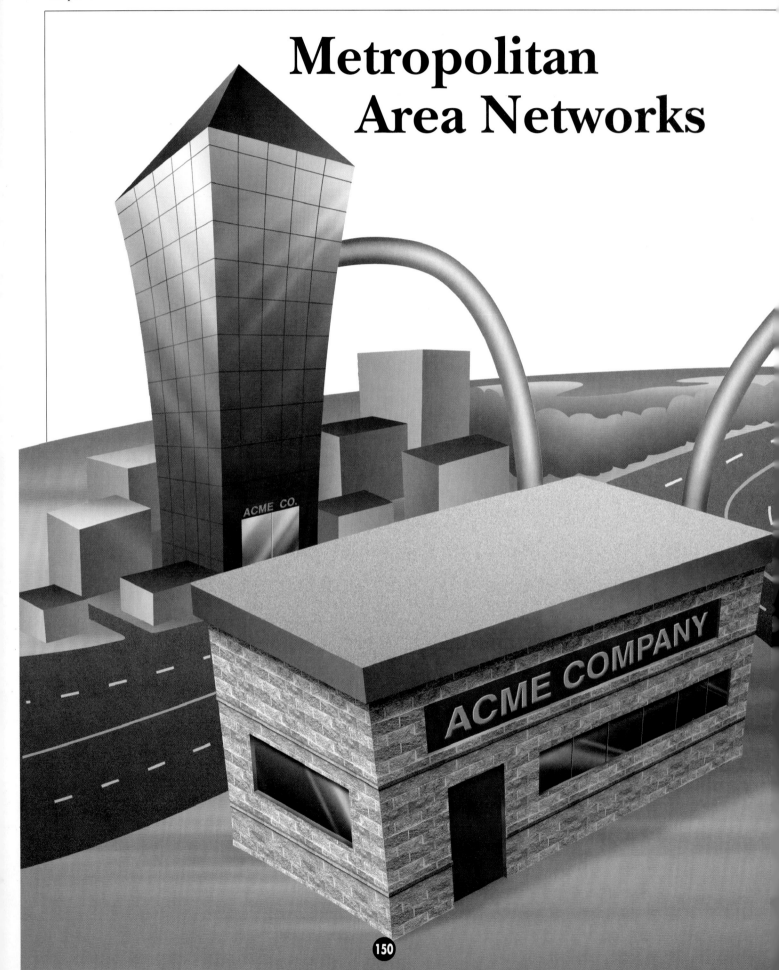

A metropolitan area network (MAN) is used to connect computer systems through a dedicated network within a city. This network could be a public offering provided by a telecommunication provider, cable television provider, or a wireless communication provider. By interconnecting many different private networks, a single, larger metropolitan area network is formed. This sometimes allows information to be shared between private enterprise and government agencies.

Wide Area Networks

Wide area networks (WANs) interconnect smaller networks. These networks can be close or at a great distance. As networks grow, more interconnections are added, increasing the size and complexity of the overall WAN. Data channels can be shared to move different types of information between two locations, or many data channels can be combined to move large amounts of data.

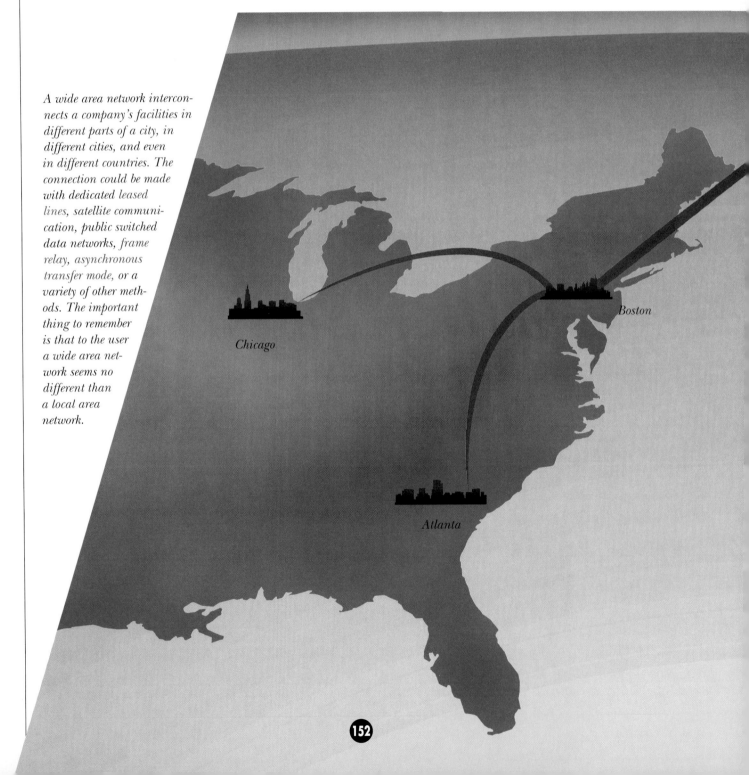

A wide area network interconnects a company's facilities in different parts of a city, in different cities, and even in different countries. The connection could be made with dedicated leased lines, satellite communication, public switched data networks, frame relay, asynchronous transfer mode, or a variety of other methods. The important thing to remember is that to the user a wide area network seems no different than a local area network.

Chicago

Boston

Atlanta

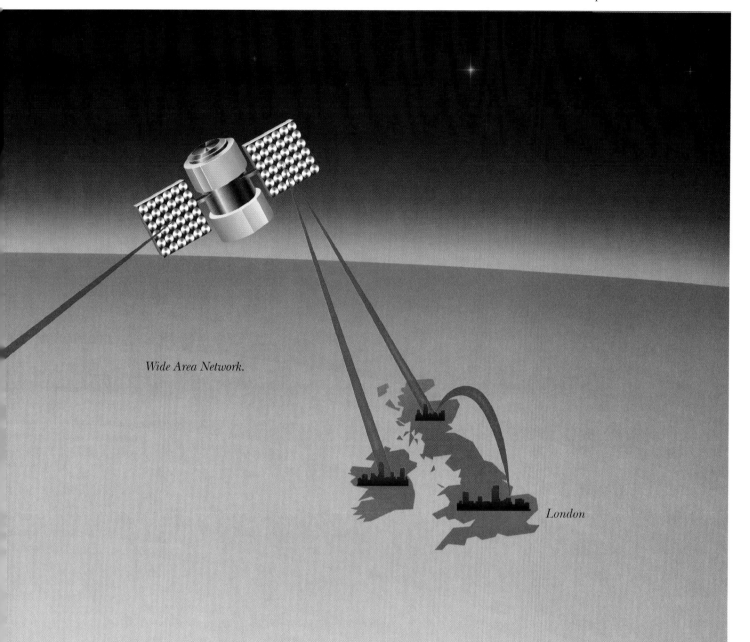

Wide Area Network.

London

Facts

Wide area networks are made up of different components. These components control how information is released onto the network, as well as network security and network access. The data is subdivided into smaller chunks to better utilize existing lines and bandwidth. Multiplexors are used in a WAN to connect local networks into global communication networks.

Point-to-Point Communication

Point-to-point communication can be used either locally or regionally. In essence, the telecommunication provider dedicates a single cable pair between the customer's two endpoints. This is an expensive alternative for wide area communications. However, with point-to-point a guaranteed response time is available and access to the network can be fully controlled. Use beyond a city boundary is usually restricted due to cost.

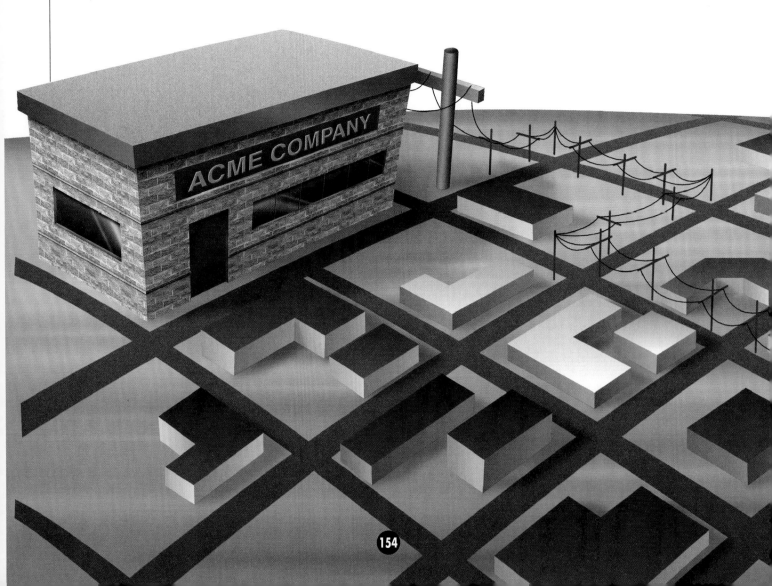

Facts

Point-to-point is like purchasing a physical set of wires from the telephone company per month. You are charged by the mile. Although the lines are very expensive, you confidently can send any information you want and you definitely can control who has access to your network.

Leased lines can provide speeds from 56 Kbps to 34 Mbps or higher. The bandwidth is dependent on the age of the telecommunication equipment available to the local provider and the cost the end-user is willing to pay. The reliability and security of a dedicated line are excellent. Security is enhanced because the customer controls who has access to the network by controlling both ends of the cable.

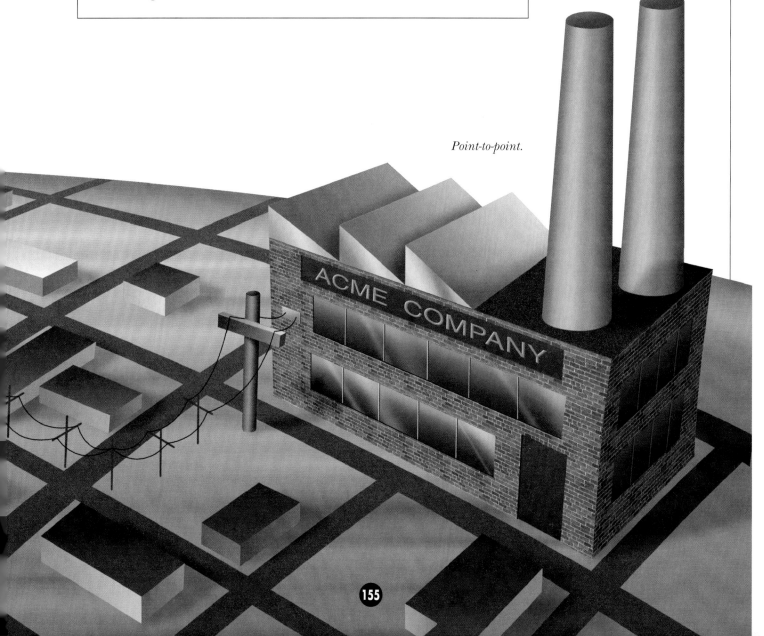

Point-to-point.

Synchronous Communication

When data is moved between points, a method of synchronizing the data is necessary. A synchronous method of data transmission requires that the network line run at a constant speed and throughput. Data is transitioned onto the network through a clocking sequence. This method of data synchronization is used in many different wide area networking applications.

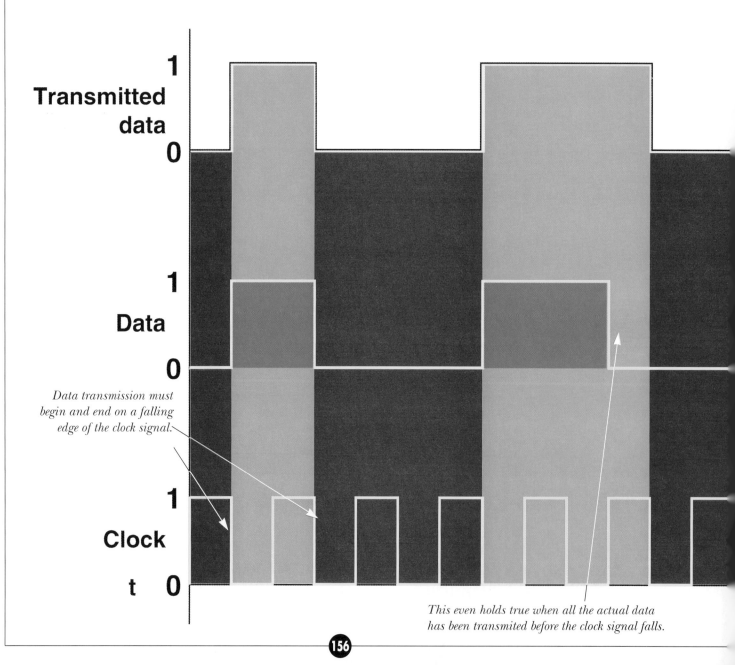

Data transmission must begin and end on a falling edge of the clock signal.

This even holds true when all the actual data has been transmited before the clock signal falls.

Facts

In synchronous communication, a special signal is used to synchronize data onto the network. This signal is a timing or reference signal and serves to set the transmission rate on the wire. This timing usually is fixed and does not increase in frequency or duty cycle. The data is synchronized with an event on the clock signal. This event is usually the falling edge of the signal. Only at that point in time will the output signal transition.

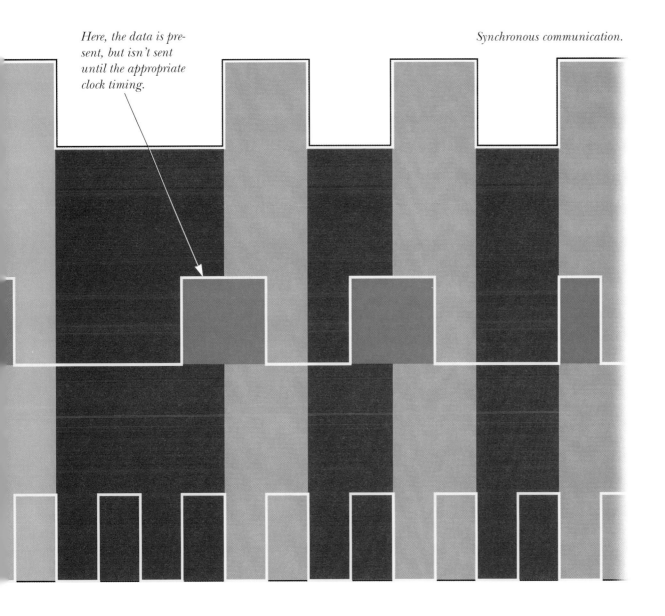

Here, the data is present, but isn't sent until the appropriate clock timing.

Synchronous communication.

Asynchronous Communication

Asynchronous communication is the method of communication most used with personal computers. This is the RS-232C protocol used by most personal computers. Data is not synchronized with the communication hardware. Instead, the bits are sent one after another. The data contains a series of predefined spaces that are used to detect a start-of-frame transition. Data rates are not always fixed. Because of lower transmission speeds, you can use normal telephone lines for asynchronous communicaton.

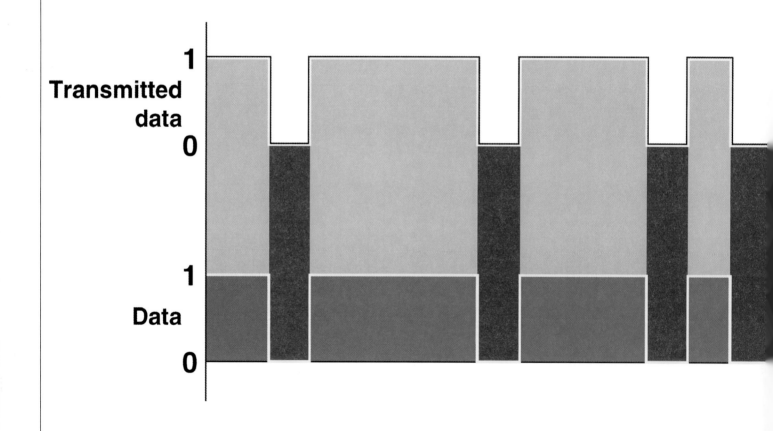

Facts

Asynchronous data communication has been used for a long time as an inexpensive means of interfacing communication hardware to computers. The data usually contains a series of events, called start and stop bits, that control how a data frame is moved between communication devices. Start-and-stop bits are a single series of bits used to identify a data transmission starting and ending to serial hardware.

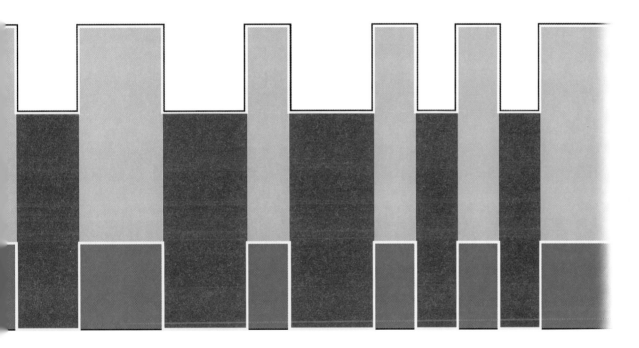

Asynchronous communication.

Modulation

Computer information must be converted from a binary state into an analog state suitable for transmission on communication equipment. This is done through modulation.

Modulation.

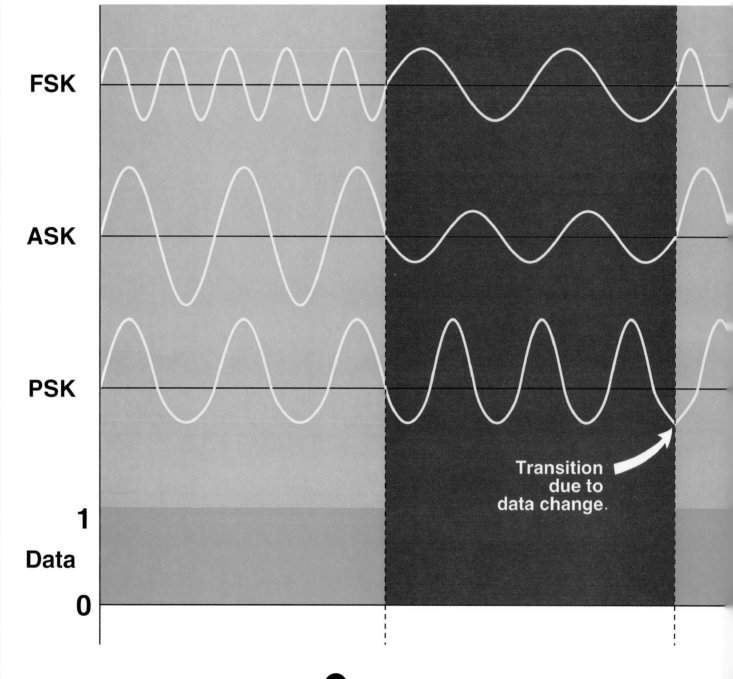

FSK

ASK

PSK

Transition due to data change.

1

Data

0

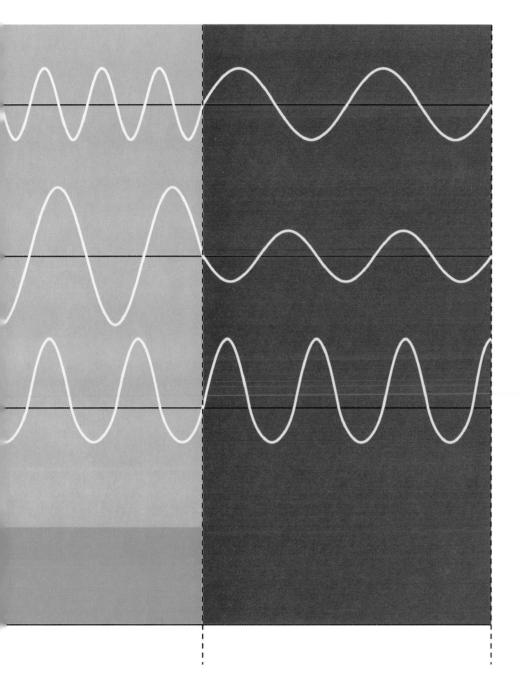

FSK (frequency shift keying) is a method of modulating a data signal by changing the frequency of the signal based on the binary data state. A logic state of '1' or TRUE would result in a brief increase in signal frequency.

ASK (amplitude shift keying) is a method of modulating a data signal by changing the amplitude of the signal. A logic state of '1' would signify an increase in signal amplitude, a logic state of '0' would result in a smaller signal. This method of modulation can be interfered with by outside interference or noise. A noise can interject increased amplitude to a signal that would result in false readings being detected.

PSK (phase shift keying) is a method of modulating a data signal by changing the phase of the signals. When a logic transition is detected, a phase shift is produced in the output signal. This is the most popular type of modulation due to increased noise immunity and reliability. This is because the receiving device is merely looking for a phase change and not trying to detect amplitude or a change in frequency.

Modems

A modem is a device used to convert digital data into analog information. The device works by modulating an output signal based on the bit level of the data. The word modem is actually two words combined, MODulator and DEModulator. The device is used in almost every type of wide area network.

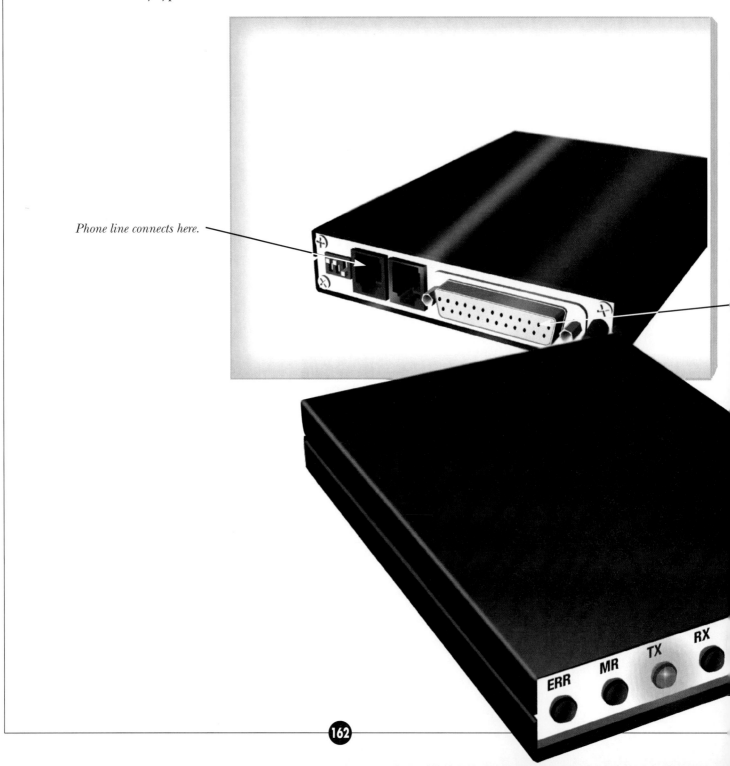

Phone line connects here.

Facts

The modem is connected to the host computer through an RS232C interface. Other modems may connect to different network devices through synchronous connections. Modems used on wide area networks almost always are connected through this type of port. A phone or public switched network connection also is needed. Most modems in use today are of the direct connect variety. A different type of modem, the acoustic type, was once popular. This type of modem required the phone handset to be inserted into a special cradle. In the future, modems that connect to cellular phones and packet telecommunication networks will be common.

RS232C port.

Modem.

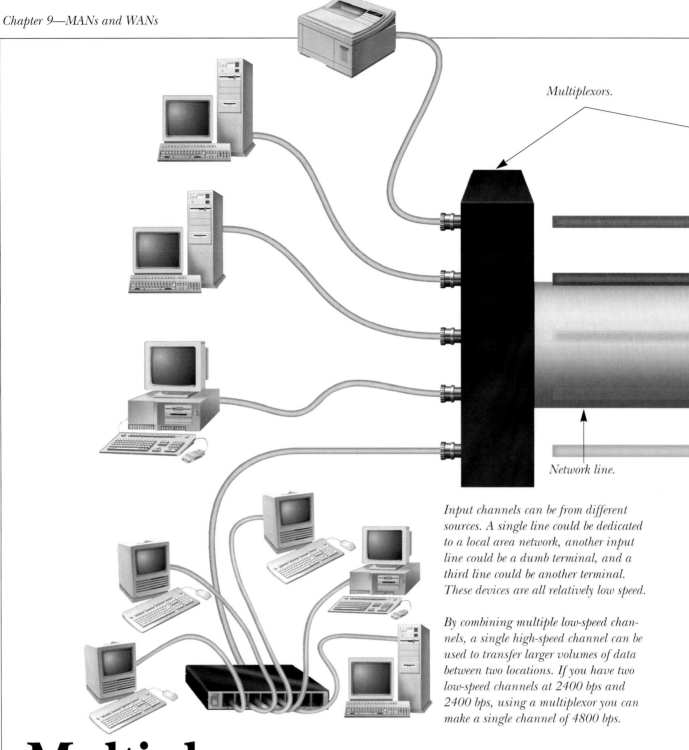

Multiplexors.

Network line.

Input channels can be from different sources. A single line could be dedicated to a local area network, another input line could be a dumb terminal, and a third line could be another terminal. These devices are all relatively low speed.

By combining multiple low-speed channels, a single high-speed channel can be used to transfer larger volumes of data between two locations. If you have two low-speed channels at 2400 bps and 2400 bps, using a multiplexor you can make a single channel of 4800 bps.

Multiplexors

A multiplexor divides a single channel into many different virtual channels. A multiplexor takes input from many low bandwidth channels and combines the information into a format that can be sent out over a single high bandwidth channel. If the multiplexor examines input lines for activity and only forwards data on active links, this is called statistical multiplexing. This method of multiplexing is in use on most commercial equipment.

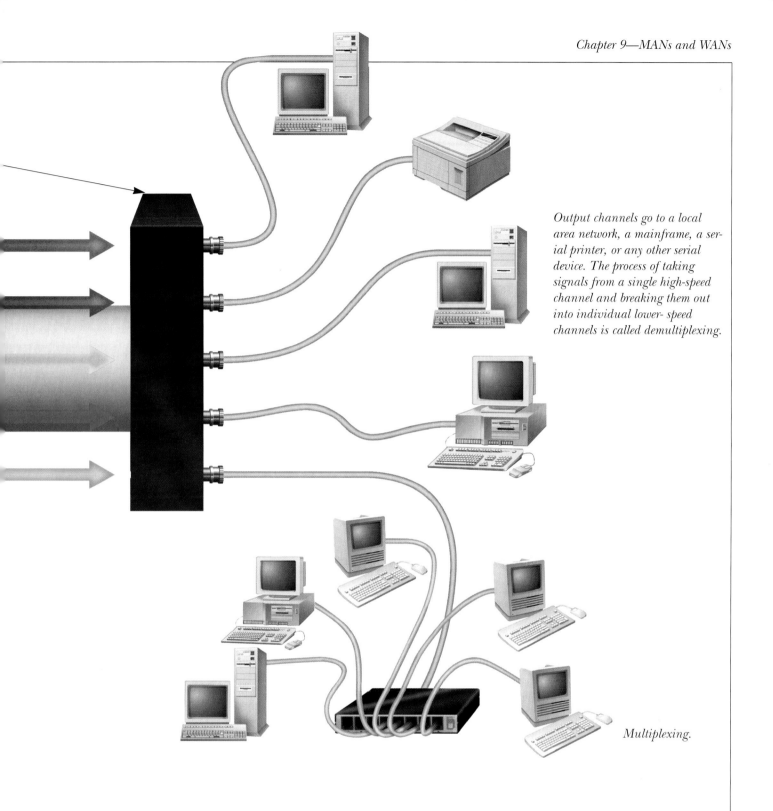

Output channels go to a local area network, a mainframe, a serial printer, or any other serial device. The process of taking signals from a single high-speed channel and breaking them out into individual lower- speed channels is called demultiplexing.

Multiplexing.

Facts

Since a multiplexor allows a single high-speed line to be used to move information, multiple slower devices can access the network. The total speed of the parts, however, cannot exceed the capacity of the network line. Most multiplexors in use today are also demultiplexors. Each port can be configured to send data and to receive it.

Time Division Multiplexing

When high speed data lines became available, a method of multiplexing signals was needed. One of the first methods used was a time division multiplexor. A time division multiplexor packs a set amount of information into each frame to be transmitted. The slower information from each channel is woven together to form a single high-speed frame.

The devices are sampled for information. As information is received, it is pieced together and then sent out over the wide area link to the destination multiplexor (mux).

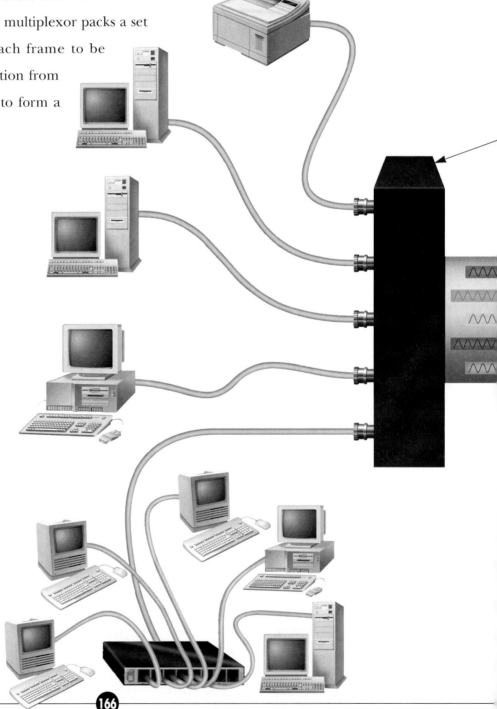

Time division multiplexing.

Facts

A time division multiplexor (TDM) combines slower channels into a single output. Here, the sum of all component channels cannot exceed the capacity of the wide area link. The time divisions must be set up the same on both muxes. A synchronous mux is a pair of muxes with a fixed time interval. An improvement of the TDM is the statistical TDM. A statistical TDM examines each channel and only sends information from active channels. This allows for higher utilization of the wide area link. Because a TDM divides time, it is the only multiplexor that can be used on a baseband line.

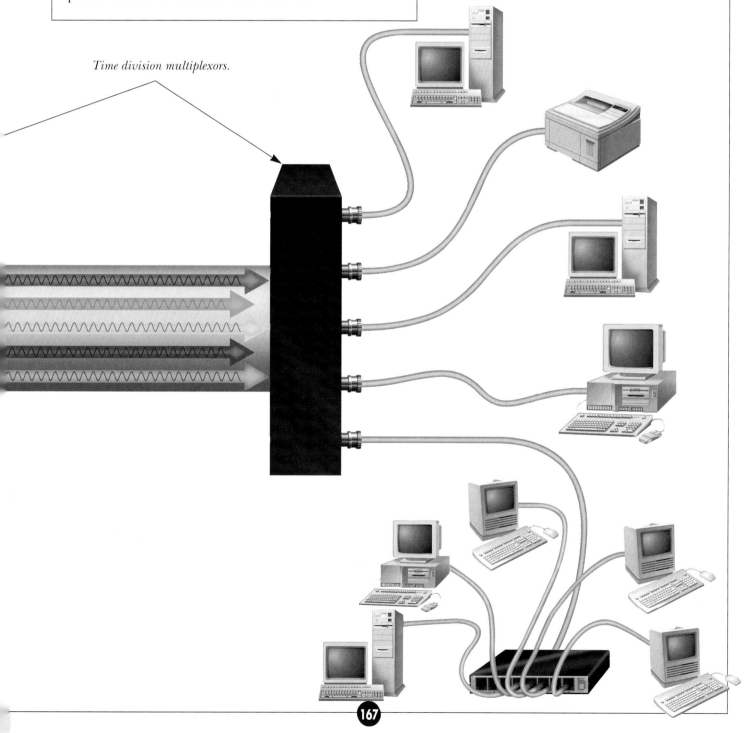

Time division multiplexors.

Frequency Division Multiplexing

A nother type of multiplexor is the frequency division multiplexor (FDM). An FDM allocates a particular frequency spectrum to each channel. This is essentially what is done with cable television. In cable television, a broadband network is used containing many different frequency channels. A typical broadcast spectrum is 800 MHz wide, which is enough room for about 80 television channels. Each channel functions separately, much like independent wires within a pair. An FDM can be used for computer networks to divide information into high-speed channels.

Each device is connected to a separate port on the FDM. Each port is assigned a separate carrier frequency. The information is then sent out over the wide area link.

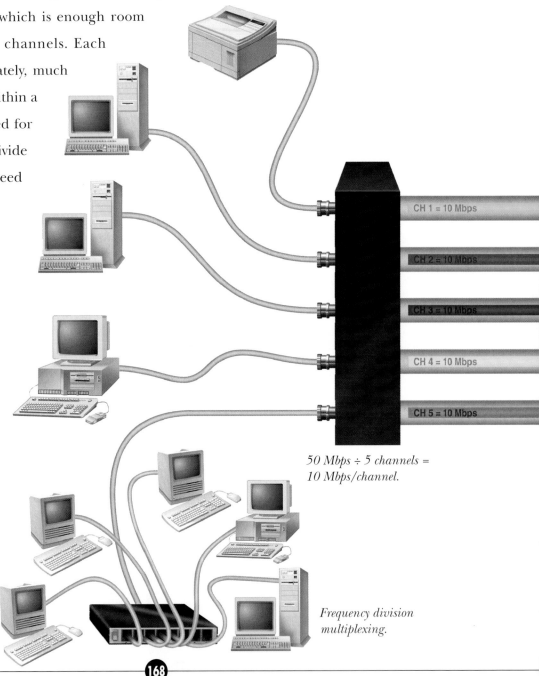

CH 1 = 10 Mbps
CH 2 = 10 Mbps
CH 3 = 10 Mbps
CH 4 = 10 Mbps
CH 5 = 10 Mbps

50 Mbps ÷ 5 channels = 10 Mbps/channel.

Frequency division multiplexing.

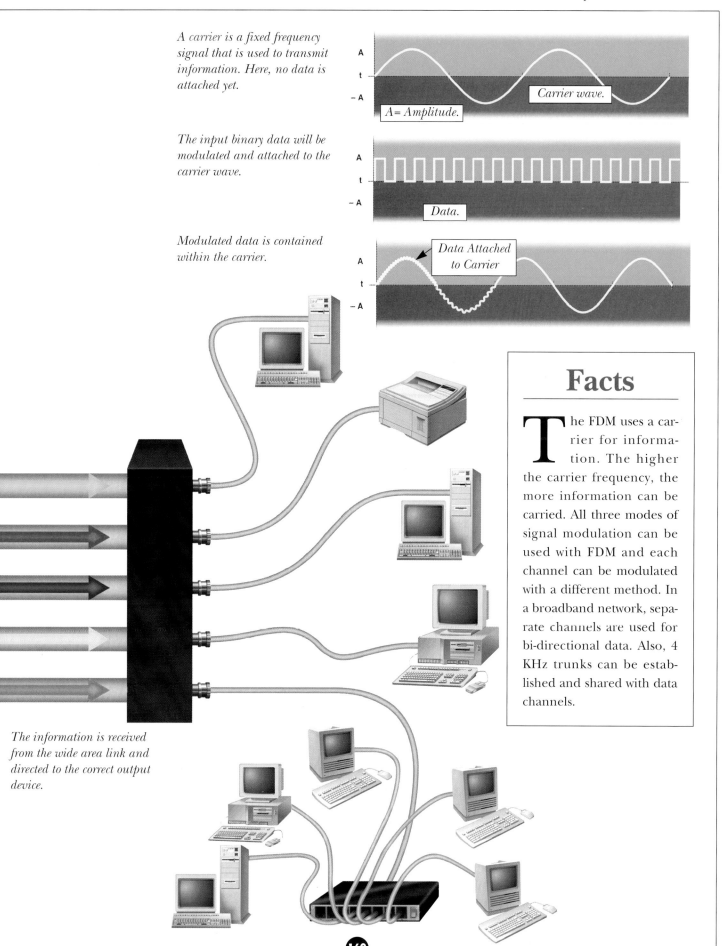

A *carrier* is a fixed frequency signal that is used to transmit information. Here, no data is attached yet.

A

t

– A

A= Amplitude.

Carrier wave.

The input binary data will be modulated and attached to the carrier wave.

A

t

– A

Data.

Modulated data is contained within the carrier.

Data Attached to Carrier

A

t

– A

Facts

The FDM uses a carrier for information. The higher the carrier frequency, the more information can be carried. All three modes of signal modulation can be used with FDM and each channel can be modulated with a different method. In a broadband network, separate channels are used for bi-directional data. Also, 4 KHz trunks can be established and shared with data channels.

The information is received from the wide area link and directed to the correct output device.

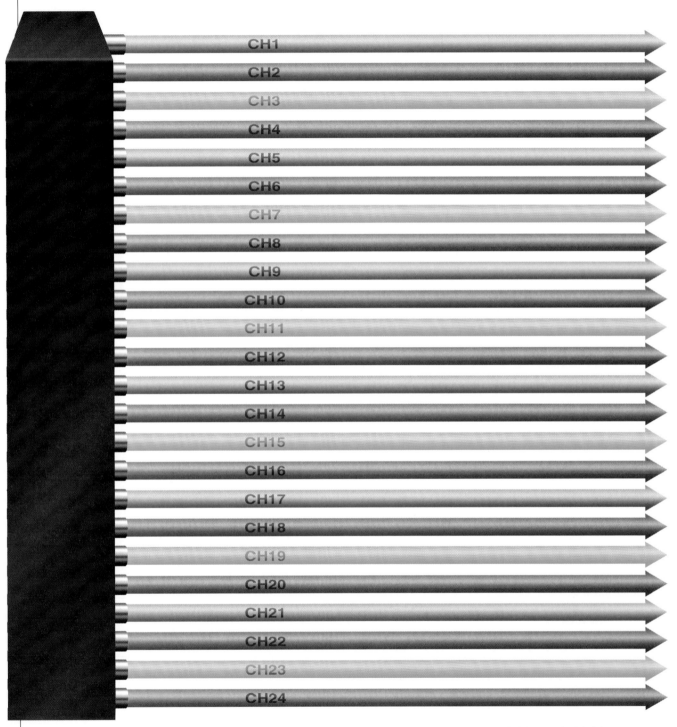

A single T1 line is divided into as many as 28 channels.

T1 and T3

The reason for all the multiplexing and modulating of signals becomes evident when a local area network is connected to a wide area network link. A typical wide area link is known as T1 or T3. These two types of line are dedicated digital channels from the telephone company's central office to your facility. Because these lines are expensive, a method of dividing a single high-speed channel into many slower-speed channels is needed.

Facts

A single T1 is capable of sending information at 1.544 Mbps. This bandwidth is divided into 28 voice channels of 64 Mbps. Each of the 28 channels has data sent in 8-bit packages and a synchronization bit is added every 193 bits.

An enhanced T1 is the T3. The T3 can transfer data at 44.54 Mbps. This is the same as multiplexing 28 T1 channels. Applications that need the throughput of T3 include medical imaging, Computer-Aided Drafting, and emerging technologies such as multimedia and video conferencing.

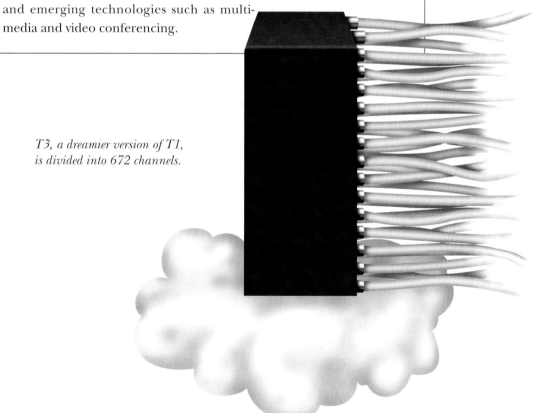

T3, a dreamier version of T1, is divided into 672 channels.

Facts

The X.25 protocol operates as a network layer protocol within the X.25 model. Operating in this realm allows for error correction and data manipulation. If a packet from a protocol such as EtherNet was sent out over a wide area link, the EtherNet data would be treated as data within an X.25 packet. The receiving host would strip off the X.25 shell and the raw EtherNet packet would then be deposited on the destination EtherNet network.

X.25

In connecting to wide area networks, most of the common protocols of TCP/IP, IPX/SPX, EtherNet, ARCnet, and Token Ring are superimposed onto a wide area protocol called X.25. The X series of standards was adopted from the Consultative Committee for International Telegraph and Telephone (CCITT). The X.25 protocol is used for the packaging and sending of data packets.

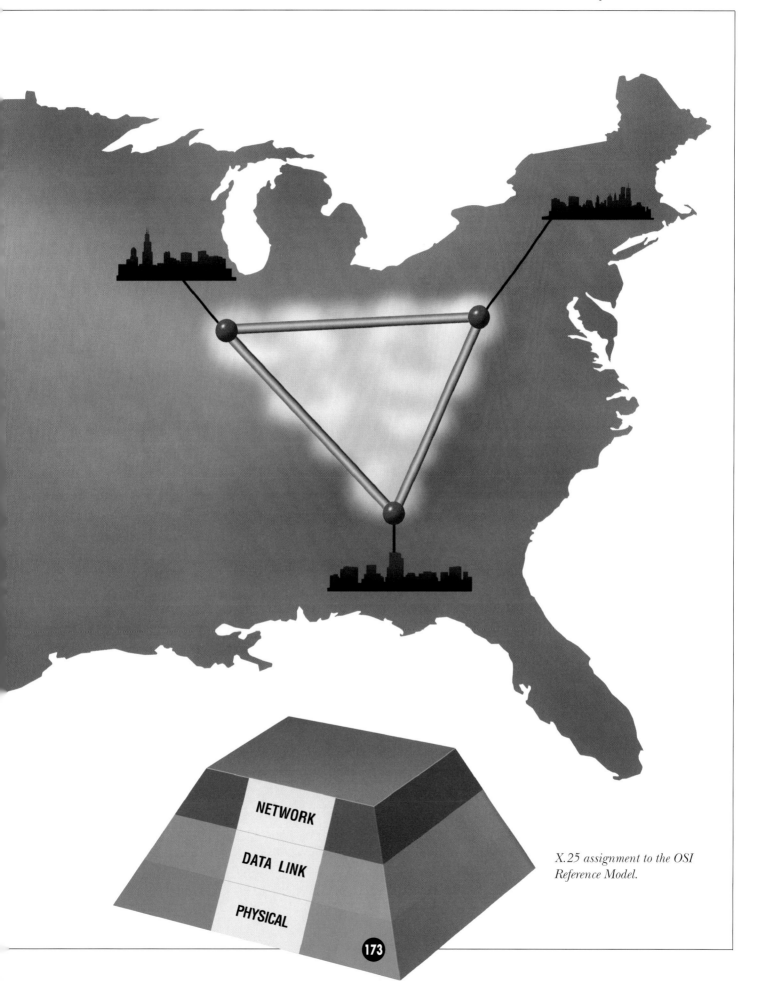

X.25 assignment to the OSI
Reference Model.

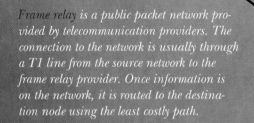

Frame relay is a public packet network provided by telecommunication providers. The connection to the network is usually through a T1 line from the source network to the frame relay provider. Once information is on the network, it is routed to the destination node using the least costly path.

After arriving at the destination switch , the data is moved onto a T1 to be sent to the destination network and node.

Frame Relay Networks

A s wide area networks became more widespread and networks became more and more interconnected, methods other than T1 connections and dedicated line connections were required. To combat the cost and the wasted bandwidth associated with the previous networks, frame relay emerged. Frame relay is a packet-based network. Information is routed to the destination through the most cost-effective path. Once information has arrived at the destination network, it then is sent out to local LANs.

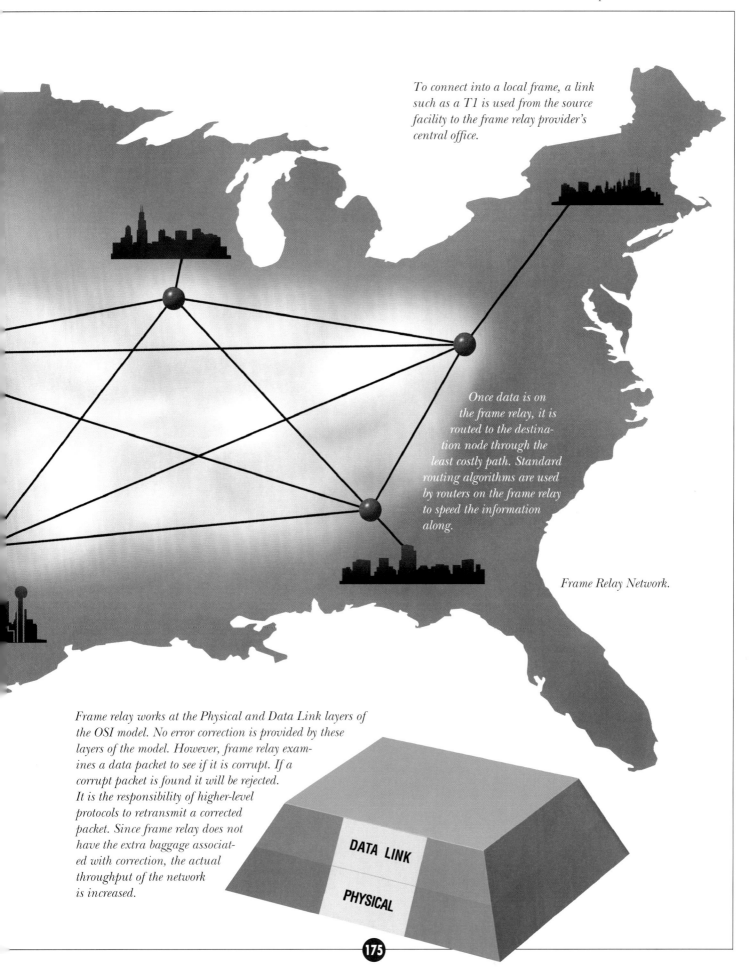

To connect into a local frame, a link such as a T1 is used from the source facility to the frame relay provider's central office.

Once data is on the frame relay, it is routed to the destination node through the least costly path. Standard routing algorithms are used by routers on the frame relay to speed the information along.

Frame Relay Network.

Frame relay works at the Physical and Data Link layers of the OSI model. No error correction is provided by these layers of the model. However, frame relay examines a data packet to see if it is corrupt. If a corrupt packet is found it will be rejected. It is the responsibility of higher-level protocols to retransmit a corrected packet. Since frame relay does not have the extra baggage associated with correction, the actual throughput of the network is increased.

DATA LINK

PHYSICAL

Data Encryption

With data being transmitted on public networks, it may be necessary for information to be changed to prevent unauthorized interception. To change data into a format that is unrecognizable by others is a process called encryption. Industries such as banking and national defense use private networks, but often use encryption anyway.

There are many different methods used for encryption. A method that is easy to decipher but illustrates the concepts behind encryption is a decoder ring found in a box of cereal. This decoder ring uses simple character substitution to encrypt a message. Substantially more elaborate methods exist that use mathematical equations and complex computer algorithms.

The message to be encoded.

Simple Substitution

A simple character substitution. This is the table used to encode the message.

A=Z	I=R	Q=J	Y=B	6=5
B=Y	J=Q	R=I	Z=A	7=4
C=X	K=P	S=H	sp=#	8=3
D=W	L=O	T=G	1=0	9=2
E=V	M=N	U=F	2=9	0=1
F=U	N=M	V=E	3=8	
G=T	O=L	W=D	4=7	
H=S	P=K	X=C	5=6	

The encoded message.

Facts

The simple example presented here illustrates the process of data encryption. Some of the more complex algorithms use statistical and mathematical analysis to encode a message. This makes the message almost impossible to decipher. An encryption method called data encryption standard (DES) is used for extremely secure data. This algorithm requires an alphanumeric string that serves as a key to encrypt and decrypt the message.

Data Compression

As applications demand higher and higher communication rates and the physical limitations of telecommunication lines are reached, a method of squeezing more out of them becomes necessary. Data compression is used to squeeze data into smaller chunks for transmission through telecommunication channels. Some data compression methods look at eliminating repetition of characters and data bits, while others use a statistical representation of a packet and reduce based on frequency of occurrence within a whole packet. If the data being transmitted is an image, then a lossy data compression method is used. This method can reduce an image considerably and not lose any perceived resolution. With lossy data compression, however, there is a net loss in data.

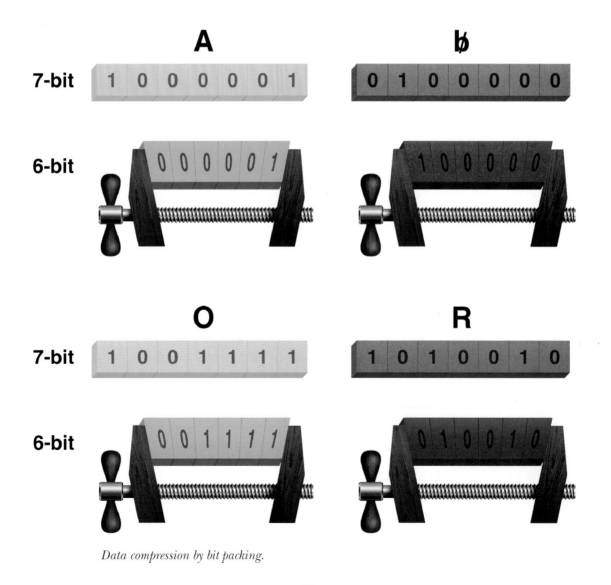

Data compression by bit packing.

Facts

A simple bit packing method of data compression can reduce a text message by as much as 15 percent. By combining this with other methods of compression, a reduction of 50 percent or more can be achieved. This type of compression is lossless since the exact message can be reproduced. Lossy compression methods should be used primarily on graphics and image data.

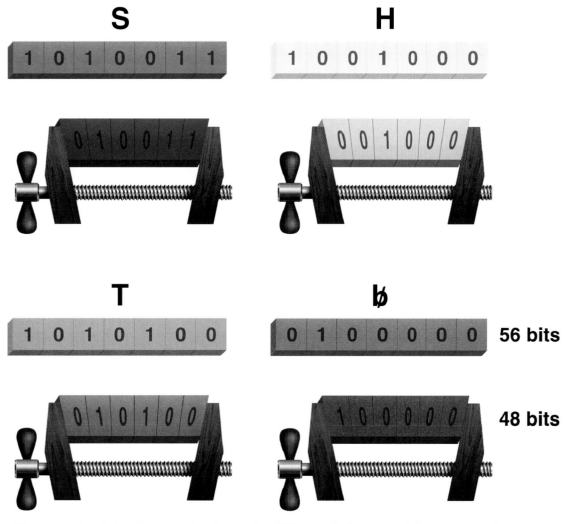

If a message is only text, then reducing the number of bits in each character code from sevven to six would result in about 15 percent compression of data.

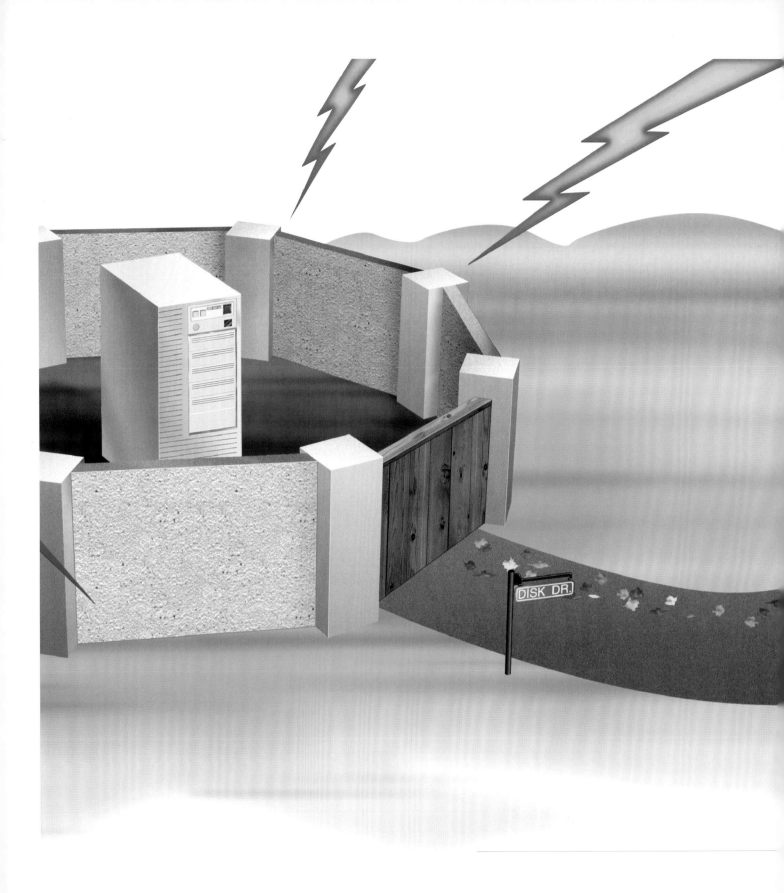

10

Protecting
Network Data

Backing Up Your Data

Backup Libraries

Tape Rotation

Server-Based Backup

Network Backup Station

Backup of Remote Workstations

Backing Up Your Data

Computer data is prone to easy loss and mistakes. A good backup of your information is vital to protect that information, whether your computer is standalone or is part of a network. To back up your computer requires some type of alternative storage. Current types of storage used to back up information are tapes, writeable optical disks, and hard disks.

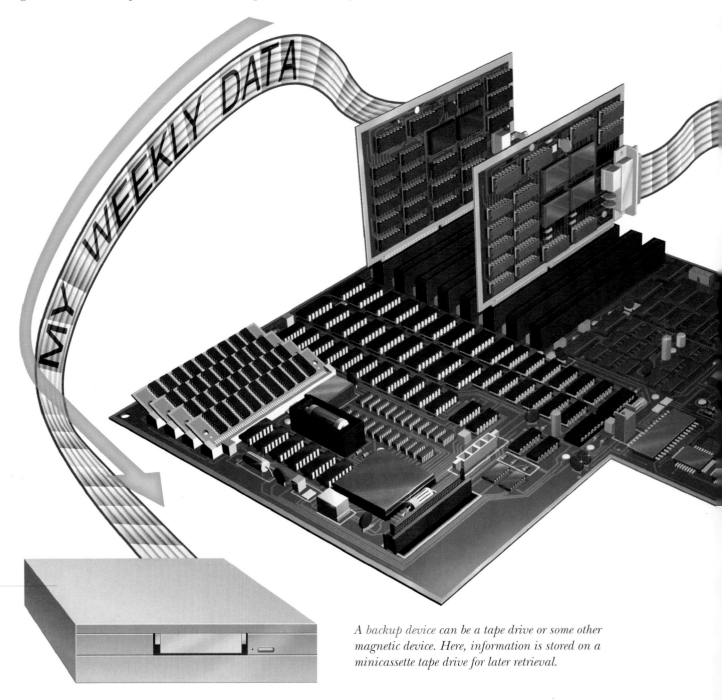

A backup device can be a tape drive or some other magnetic device. Here, information is stored on a minicassette tape drive for later retrieval.

Facts

The current trend toward bigger and faster hard drives has resulted in a need to back up large amounts of information. In the past, a hard disk was backed up to 10 or 20 floppy disks, but today a backup can easily require hundreds or thousands of floppies. To address the problem of large disk backup, tape drives have been adapted to smaller personal computers. Tape drives are manufactured with capacities that correlate directly to disk drive capacities. It isn't a problem to find standard tape drive capacities of 120M, 250M, 1G, 2G, or 4G. The capacities indicate how much information can be stored on a single tape cartridge or cassette.

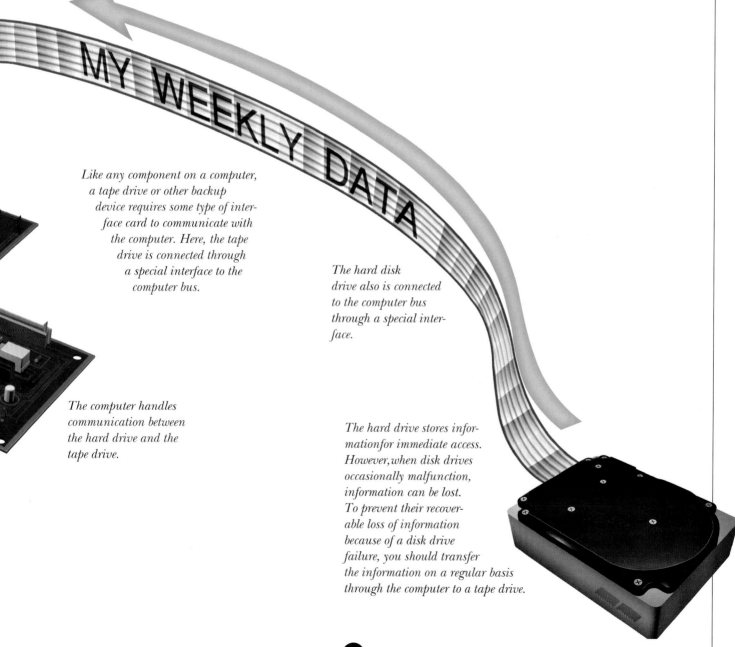

Like any component on a computer, a tape drive or other backup device requires some type of interface card to communicate with the computer. Here, the tape drive is connected through a special interface to the computer bus.

The hard disk drive also is connected to the computer bus through a special interface.

The computer handles communication between the hard drive and the tape drive.

The hard drive stores information for immediate access. However, when disk drives occasionally malfunction, information can be lost. To prevent their recoverable loss of information because of a disk drive failure, you should transfer the information on a regular basis through the computer to a tape drive.

Information is stored in a backup library. This backup library allows individual files to be referenced in a single package. The backup library contains additional information such as error-correction information, revision history, and file locations within the backup library. The error correction information is used to re-create files if the backup library is corrupted. The file locations are necessary to restore individual files from the tape drive to the destination hard disk.

Backup Libraries

Information to be stored on tape is usually stored in a special format. Individual files from the hard drive are stored in groupings called save sets, backup libraries, or archive collections. Although different computer systems and manufacturers use different names for these libraries, most information on tape is stored in much the same format.

The files are stored on a disk drive in many different locations.

Facts

To back up information from a hard drive to a tape drive usually requires special software. This software reads the disk directory or file structure and then builds a backup library on tape with the same structure. Information is then transferred from disk to tape and is appended at the end of the directory structure. After an entry is written, special information also may be written to the tape that allows re-creation of the backed-up data to a disk drive. If a problem occurs, the data is available on the backup tape cartridge.

Tape Rotation

When you back up information to tape, you should use different tape cartridges for each backup, and keep older backup versions on hand. Of course, buying new tape cartridges each time you want to perform a backup could become expensive, so you can rotate your cartridges to protect the data and still allow reuse of the cartridges. Several different tape rotation schemes exist. The most common is the grandfather method, which often is used by network file servers.

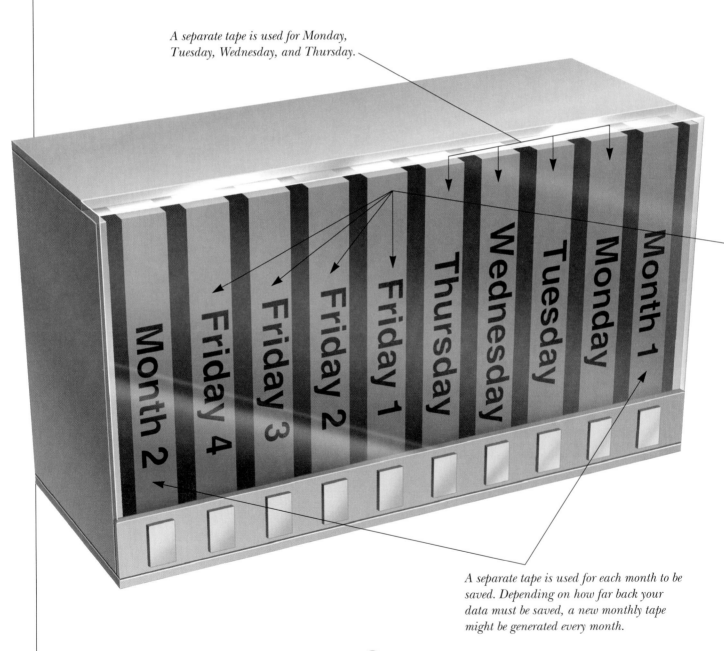

A separate tape is used for Monday, Tuesday, Wednesday, and Thursday.

A separate tape is used for each month to be saved. Depending on how far back your data must be saved, a new monthly tape might be generated every month.

DAILY	DAILY	DAILY	DAILY	WEEKLY	MONTHLY
Monday	Tuesday	Wednesday	Thursday	Friday1	
Monday	Tuesday	Wednesday	Thursday	Friday2	
Monday	Tuesday	Wednesday	Thursday	Friday3	
Monday	Tuesday	Wednesday	Thursday	Friday4	
					Month1
Monday	Tuesday	Wednesday	Thursday	Friday1	
Monday	Tuesday	Wednesday	Thursday	Friday2	
Monday	Tuesday	Wednesday	Thursday	Friday3	
Monday	Tuesday	Wednesday	Thursday	Friday4	
Monday	Tuesday	Wednesday	Thursday	Friday5	
					Month2

A separate tape is used for each Friday in a month; these are labeled Friday1, Friday2, Friday3, Friday4, and if a fifth week is present in a month, Friday5.

TIP: *It makes the backup process quicker if you first make sure all files that are unnecessary have been removed from your directory structure. There's no sense backing up garbage files or temporary files that will never be needed again.*

Facts

The actual number of tapes needed each day is based on the available disk capacity, the number of changed files each day, and the capacity of your tape drive. A separate tape is needed for each day of the week, and this one set of Monday through Thursday tapes is reused every week. The Friday tape contains a complete backup of everything that has changed from Monday morning through Friday at backup time. The monthly tape contains information as it stands at the end of the entire month.

Server-Based Backup

To back up a file server requires a local tape drive of sufficient capacity to transfer the local disk volumes to tape in a time-efficient manner. The backup occurs over the local computer bus and usually is done after the last workstation user logs off for the day.

The network file server contains the hardware and network operating system.

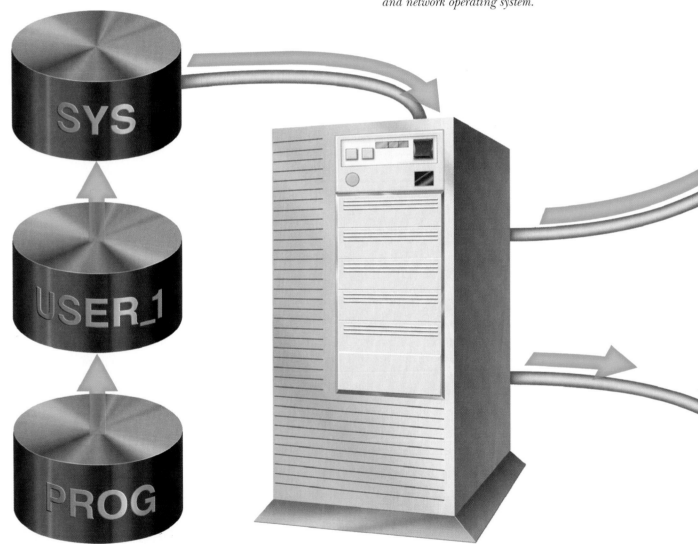

The network disk volumes store information that needs to be backed up to tape. This information is transferred by the local computer through internal interface cards to the local tape drive(s).

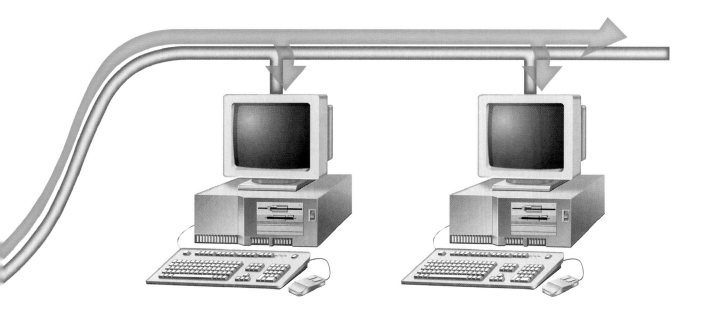

Facts

The server-based backup uses hardware within the file server to back up disk volumes. The backup usually results in the file server being unavailable to network users. To back up information also requires a special program that can control the tape drive, which is written especially for the network operating system in use. This type of backup usually requires a network administrator or manager to be present during the operation.

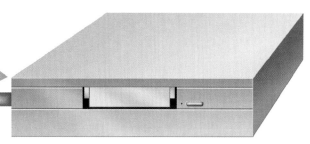

The local tape drive(s) must be accessible via commands at the file server to accept information from the network disk volumes.

Network Backup Station

Another method of backing up a file server is to use a workstation on the LAN and designate it as a backup station. This allows network backups to be scheduled on a regular basis. The backups usually can be done without operator intervention. In this backup scheme, a tape drive is placed within a remote workstation and information is transferred across the network onto the tape drive.

The network file server contains the disk drives to be backed up. The actual backup path is through the LAN to the remote workstations.

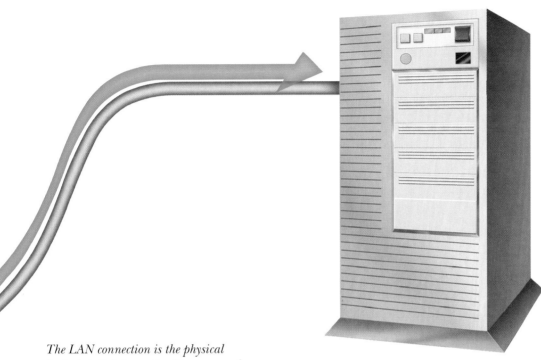

The LAN connection is the physical backup path between the file server and backup station.

Facts

A key advantage of the network backup station is that it can be used by more than one file server, resulting in less hardware and a more cost-effective configuration. An even bigger advantage is that it usually allows the file server to be backed up without taking down the file servers or disabling user access to the servers.

This tape drive would be part of this backup section.

The network backup station contains at least one local tape drive to back up the remote file servers.

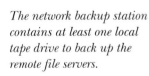

Backup station.

Backup of Remote Workstations

Another important backup operation is to back up individual workstations. The backup process allows the workstations to be placed in a special host mode that allows the workstation disk drive to be accessed by the file server or backup station. The information can be transferred directly from the workstation's disk to tape by the file server. The tape drive places the backed-up files onto magnetic data cartridges.

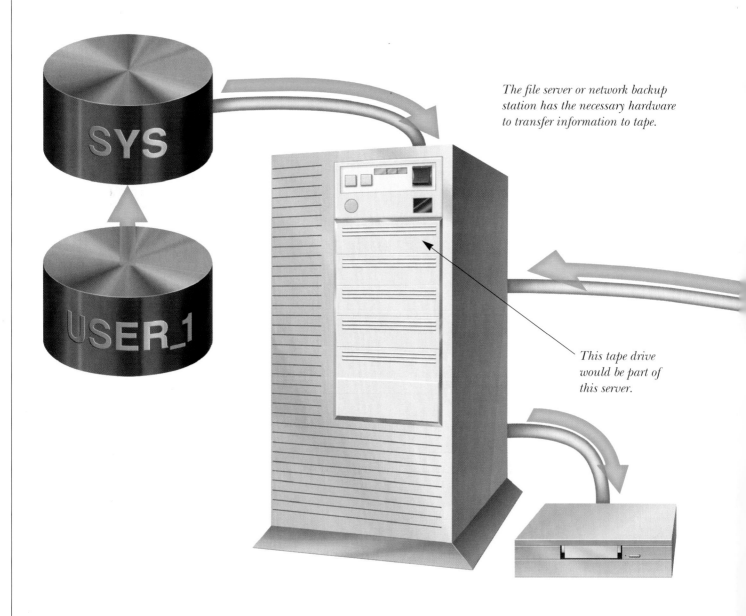

The file server or network backup station has the necessary hardware to transfer information to tape.

This tape drive would be part of this server.

Facts

The backup of remote workstations to a LAN device is a cost-effective method of backing up individual workstations. The information is transferred to a local tape drive from the remote file server or workstation. Special software on the workstations and file server allows the local hard drives on each workstation to be shared.

The workstation to be backed up is usually placed in a special mode by the user or network administrator. This special mode allows the workstation's hard drives to be accessed by other network stations. Some NOS allow multiple workstations to access a workstation in backup mode, but other NOS allow only the server.

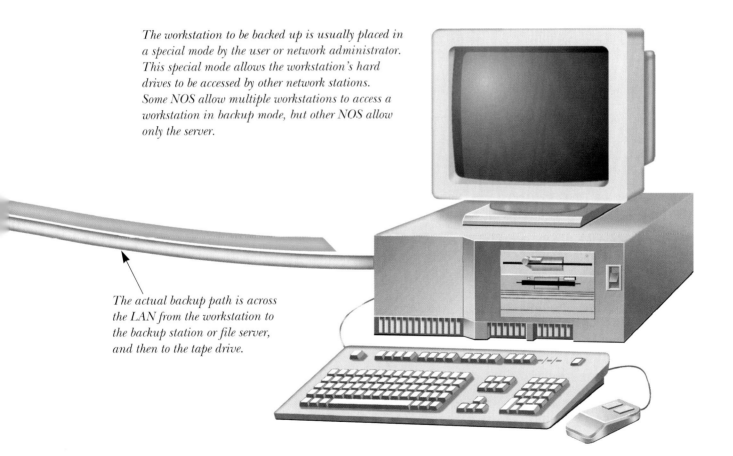

The actual backup path is across the LAN from the workstation to the backup station or file server, and then to the tape drive.

GLOSSARY

10BASET EtherNet protocol on unshielded twisted pair cabling. See "Star Topology" in Chapter 4.

access control database A file that contains security information such as user names and passwords. See "Access Control" in Chapter 7.

access control The process of controlling how a computer or device is used. See "Access Control" in Chapter 7.

ACK (Acknowledge) A positive response to a handshaking request. Also, an acknowledge packet in some token networking protocols. See "ARCnet Network" in Chapter 6.

active Electronic components or circuit that modifies a signal through amplification, attenuation, or other methods of signal conditioning. See "Network Interconnection" in Chapter 5.

air plenum Space found in heating ducts, walls, and above dropped ceilings. See "Coaxial Cable" in Chapter 5.

alert field The preamble field in an ARCnet network packet. See "ARCnet Network" in Chapter 6.

antenna A device used to send electromagnetic energy through the atmosphere. See "Wireless LANs" in Chapter 4.

Application Layer The layer of the OSI model that specifies how user interfaces and end-user programs are to communicate with the network. See "Introduction to the OSI MODEL" in Chapter 3.

application program A computer program that allows a user to perform a specific task. See "How A Network Operating System Works" in Chapter 7.

archive collection See *backup library.*

ASCII American Standard Code for Information Interchange. The character set used in all personal computers. See "Character Sets" in Chapter 1.

ASK Amplitude Shift Keying. Modulating a carrier wave by changing its amplitude. See "Modulation" in Chapter 9.

asynchronous Communication signals that are not time-dependent. See "Asynchronous Communication" in Chapter 9.

asynchronous server A network device that has serial ports for the connection of modems, terminals, and output devices to share these resources between host systems and workstations. See "Saving through Device Sharing," in Chapter 2.

AUI See *attachment unit interface.*

attachment unit interface A connector on EtherNet devices such as NIC's, terminal servers, repeaters, bridges, etc that is used with transceiver cables. See "Network Interface Cards," in Chapter 5.

authentication Identification of a user to determine the user's right to access a network device, file, or other object. See "File Server Login" in Chapter 2.

backbone The primary network cable or network trunk off of which workstation and hubs are usually interconnected. See "Bus Topology" in Chapter 4.

backup device A tape drive, hard disk drive, floppy disk drive, or any other device to which information is written for archiving purposes. See "Backing Up Your Data" in Chapter 10.

backup library A special file used in data archives that contains a group of data files, error correction information, security information, and other information that allows a single file—or the whole group of files—to be

restored to the primary disk volume. See "Backing Up Your Data" in Chapter 10.

backup station A special workstation on a network which is set up to perform archiving operations. This workstation can service one or more file servers. See "Network Backup Station" in Chapter 10.

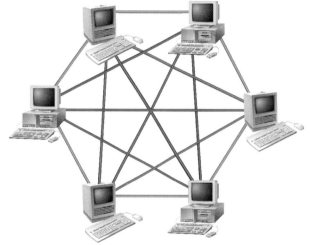

binary Having two possible values. Binary numbers, each with a possible value of 0 or 1, are used in the Base 2 number system. In digital circuits, being ON yields a logical value of 1, and being OFF yields a logical value of 0. See "Character Sets" in Chapter 1.

BNC connector A type of connector commonly used at the ends of coaxial cable. See "Coaxial Cable Connectors" in Chapter 5.

boot PROM A program stored in hardware that allows a computer to request that its operating system be loaded over the network instead of from a local hard drive or floppy drive. See "Network Interface Cards" in Chapter 5.

bridge A network device that connects similar architecture networks together. A bridge operates on physical addresses within a network. See "Bridges" in Chapter 8.

brouter A combination network device that exhibits functionality of both a network bridge and a network router. See "Bridges" in Chapter 8.

bus topology A network topology that physically interconnects workstations and network devices in parallel on a network segment. See "Bus Topology" in Chapter 4.

cable A wire or other device designed to carry information. See "Sharing on a Network" in Chapter 1.

cable pair Two wires, usually twisted. See "Star Topology" in Chapter 4.

cache A special memory buffer designed to hold information that needs to be accessed often. Caches are most often used to increase performance of slow devices such as disk drives. See "Server-Based LANs" in Chapter 7.

carrier A sinusoidal signal to which information is attached for transmission. See "Frequency Division Multiplexing" in Chapter 9.

Category 3 UTP cable designed for data and voice communication of 10 Mbps. See "Unshielded Twisted Pair Cable" in Chapter 5.

Category 4 UTP cable designed for data and voice communication of 16 Mbps. See "Unshielded Twisted Pair Cable" in Chapter 5.

Category 5 UTP cable designed for voice and data communications to 100 Mbps. See "Unshielded Twisted Pair Cable" in Chapter 5.

CATV Cable television. See "Baseband Network Communication" in Chapter 1.

CCITT See *Comité Consultatif International Téléphonique et Télégraphique.*

central processing unit The brain of a computer. This unit is responsible for all logical and arithmetic processing. See "Network Workstations" in Chapter 1.

central office The local switching hub for a telephone exchange. See "Star Topology" in Chapter 4.

checksum An error-checking technique in which the number of bits in a unit of data is summed and transmitted along with the data. The receiving computer then checks the sum of the bits of data it receives. If the numbers differ, a transmission error probably has occurred. See "TCP/IP" in Chapter 6, and "OSI Media Layers" in Chapter 3.

cladding Material that surronds the core of a fiber-optic cable. See "Fiber-Optic Cable and Connections" in Chapter 5.

client/server A distributed computing model that uses a central computer called a server for shared information, and local workstations called clients for local processing. See "SPX/IPX" in Chapter 6.

coaxial cable Cable that contains a center conductor surrounded by an insulator. The insulator has a concentric shield of braided wire, foil, or both. Used in communication and networking. See "Coaxial Cable" in Chapter 5.

Comité Consultatif International Téléphonique et Télégraphique The Consultative Committee for International Telegraph and Telephone, an international organization that sets standards for analog and digital communications. See "X.25" in Chapter 9.

command interpreter The part of an operating system that serves as an interface between the user and other operating system functions. See "Single-User Operating Systems" in Chapter 7.

communication protocol A specific set of instructions and data structures used by devices that need to exchange information. See "Introduction to OSI MODEL" in Chapter 3.

compression See *data compression.*

computer bus The device within a computer used to interconnect the processor and

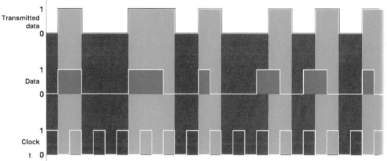

peripheral components such as disk drives, graphics hardware, tape drives, and network adapter cards. See "Network Workstations" in Chapter 1.

computer virus A program that is designed to cause problems in a computer, and which often is intended to propagate from computer to computer. These programs can be extremely destructive. See "Virus Protection" in Chapter 2.

concentrator A network device that combines incoming messages into a single message. See "Network Interconnection" in Chapter 5.

conductor Something that allows electrons to move; a wire. See "Coaxial Cable" in Chapter 5.

connection-oriented communications A network transaction that verifies data delivery and proper sequencing of delivered data. This is accomplished by the exchange of handshaking information. See "SPX/IPX" in Chapter 6.

connectionless A network transaction where the transaction is not acknowledged by the receiving source. See "SPX/IPX" in Chapter 6.

connector A device used at the end of a wire or cable that allows the wire or cable to be connected to other equipment, or even to

other wires or cables. See "Coaxial Cable Connectors" in Chapter 5.

control character One of a set of characters which serve to control specific functions when they are interpreted by printers and terminals. Examples are form feed, line feed, carriage return, and so on. See "Character Sets" in Chapter 1.

CDDI Copper Distributed Data Interface. FDDI protocols over unshielded twisted pair. See "FDDI" in Chapter 6.

core The center of fiber-optic cable. See "Fiber Optic Cable and Connectors" in Chapter 5.

CPU See *central processing unit.*

CRC See *cyclic redundancy check.*

cyclic redundancy check An error correction code based on a mathematical polynomial. See "OSI Media Layers" in Chapter 3 and "ARCnet Network" in Chapter 6.

data compression A method of data reduction by examining the raw data for repeatable patterns of bits, characters, or expressions, and then substituting a single simplified expression that requires less storage. See "OSI Host Layers" in Chapter 3 and "Data Compression" in Chapter 9.

data encryption standard A method of data security adopted by the United States government. See "Data Encryption" in Chapter 9.

data switch A network device that connects different network segments based on data packet addressing. See "Data Switches" in Chapter 8.

demodulator A device that removes data from a wave and converts it to digital format. See "Modems" in Chapter 9.

DES See *data encryption standard.*

device driver A program that communicates with computer hardware and with the computer operating system. See "How A Network Operating System Works" in Chapter 7.

direct memory access A method of transferring information between computer memory and peripheral devices without the aid of the CPU. See "Network Workstations" in Chapter 1.

DMA See *direct memory access.*

duty cycle A ratio of on time verses off time of an electrical signal. See "Synchronous Communication" in Chapter 9.

EBCDIC Extended binary-coded decimal interchange code. An eight-bit character code system used mostly on IBM mainframes. See "Character Sets" in Chapter 1.

ECC See *error correction code.*

electrical isolation Preventing the flow of electrons between two systems. This is usually accomplished through some method of optical coupling. See "Fiber-Optic Cable and Connectors" in Chapter 5.

electronic mail A method of exchanging messages, reports, or other information between network users. See "Campus Network" in Chapter 1.

encryption Changing a message or a data file into a format that is unreadable unless decrypted. See *DES* and "OSI Host Layers" in Chapter 3.

EOT End of transmission. An ASCII control code used to signal the end of a message. See "ARCnet Network" in Chapter 6.

error checking Hardware or software that determines whether or not a message is corrupted. See "Token-Based Networks" in Chapter 6.

error correction Hardware or software that can repair a corrupted message. See "OSI Host Layers" in Chapter 3.

error correction code A special code that is generated in hardware to indicate if a network packet is corrupt. The code received with the network packet is compared to the code generated on the local system. If the codes match, then no error is present. See "OSI Media Layers" in Chapter 3.

extended LAN A network that interconnects more than one facility. See "Repeaters" in Chapter 8.

falling edge The transition of a binary signal from a logical high to a logical zero state. See "Synchronous Communication" in Chapter 9.

FDDI See *Fiber Distributed Data Interface.*

FDM See *Frequency Division Multiplexor.*

Fiber Distributed Data Interface. A 100 Mbps network that uses fiber-optic cable. See "FDDI" in Chapter 6.

fiber-optic cable A collection of glass fiber used to transmit voice and data information. See "Fiber-Optic Cable and Connectors" in Chapter 5.

fiber optics A technology concerned with the transmission of data by light through glass. See "Fiber-Optic Cable and Connectors" in Chapter 5.

file server A central computer that offers disk storage and file sharing over a network. See "A Basic Network" in Chapter 1.

filter To remove or separate electrical noise from an electrical signal. To remove or separate selected data from a data file. See "Network Interconnection" in Chapter 5.

flow control Control of data transfer. See "OSI Host Layers" in Chapter 3.

frame A collection of data, tokens, or control packets that are to be transmitted over a network. See "OSI Media Layers" in Chapter 3.

frame relay A wide-area networking topology. See "Frame Relay Networks" in Chapter 9.

frequency division multiplexor A method of breaking a network line into many different frequency channels. See "Frequency Division Multiplexing" in Chapter 9.

gateway A device that interconnects two networks of different architecture and technology. See "Gateways" in Chapter 8.

grandfather method A backup rotation method. This is a method of rotating backup media to insure against data loss. See "Tape Rotation" in Chapter 10.

ground potential Electrical signal referenced to the earth. See "Coaxial Cable" in Chapter 5.

host address field The source network address of a network message. See "OSI Media Layers" in Chapter 3.

hub A network device that allows one or more network devices, typically workstations, to be interconnected to a network backbone. See "Star Topology" in Chapter 4 and "Network Interconnection" in Chapter 5.

IEEE See *Institute of Electrical and Electronic Engineers.*

IEEE 802.3 The specification dealing with EtherNet networks. See "EtherNet" in Chapter 6.

IEEE 802.5 The specification dealing with token passing networks. See "Token Ring" in Chapter 6.

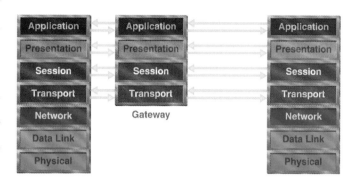

impedance An electrical measurement of how much a signal will be restricted by a device that prevents electron flow. This measurement takes into account the frequency of the signal as well as the type of device causing the restriction in flow. See "Coaxial Cable" in Chapter 5.

input/output port A method of bringing data into and sending data out of a computer. See "Network Interface Cards" in Chapter 5.

interference A disruption of an electrical signal. This may come from lights, electric motors, or any other electrical source. See "Coaxial Cable" in Chapter 5.

internetwork A wide-area network comprised of more than one network connected to function as one larger network. See "TCP/IP" in Chapter 6.

interrupt An event requiring immediate attention that is sent to the CPU by a NIC, serial port, or other peripheral device. See "Network Interface Cards" in Chapter 5 and "Peer-To-Peer LANs" in Chapter 7.

IP address Internet Protocol node identification. This is a 32-bit value used to uniquely identify a network device. See "Routers" in Chapter 8.

ISO International Standards Organization. See "Introduction to the OSI Model" in Chapter 3.

ITT Invitation To Transmit. See "ARCnet Network" in Chapter 6.

kernel The part of an operating system that provides basic functions. See "How A Network Operating System Works" in Chapter 7.

kevlar A strong plastic material used in fiber-optic cables and bulletproof vests. See "Fiber-Optic Cable and Connectors" in Chapter 5.

LAN See *local area network.*

leased line A communication line obtained from a local telecommunications provider that is connected between multiple facilities of an organization. See "Point-to-Point Communication" in Chapter 9.

LED Light Emitting Diode. The colored indicator lights on the front of computers and computer boards. See "Network Interconnection" in Chapter 5.

line cost A value assigned by the network administrator to a particular network path. See "Routers" in Chapter 8.

local area network Computers that interconnect to share information and programs.

logical address A high-level workstation address assigned by many networking protocols. See "Routers" in Chapter 8.

lossless A type of data compression that allows all original data to be decompressed. See "Data Compression" in Chapter 9.

lossy A method of data compression that results in a net loss of information. Typically, this method is used for image and video data. See "Data Compression" in Chapter 9.

MAU media access unit. See "Network Interconnection" in Chapter 5.

Mbps Megabits per second. See "Data Transfer Rate" in Chapter 1.

memory The part of the computer used to store programs and data for immediate access by the CPU. See "Network Interface Cards" in Chapter 5.

mesh A networking topology that requires all network devices to have dedicated paths to all other devices on that network. See "Wiring with Efficiency" in Chapter 4.

MAN Metropolitan Area Network. See "Metropolitan Area Networks" in Chapter 9.

micron

A unit of measure equal to one-millionth of a meter. See "Fiber-Optic Connections" in Chapter 5.

modulation Placing information onto a carrier wave. See "Modulation" in Chapter 9.

modulator A device that places information onto a carrier wave. See "Modems" in Chapter 9.

Motif A user interface and programming environment for use with X-window systems. See "OSI Host Layers" in Chapter 3.

mux An abbreviation for multiplexor.

multitasking Running more than one computer application at a time. See "Comparison of Single-User Operating Systems and NOS" in Chapter 7.

NAK Negative acknowledge. See "ARCnet Network" in Chapter 6.

network A connection of workstations and devices for the purpose of sharing resources and exchanging information. See "A Basic Network" in Chapter 1.

network file system The remote disk service and file sharing protocol defined for the TCP/IP suite of protocols. See "TCP/IP" in Chapter 6 and "OSI Host Layers" in Chapter 3.

network interface card The circuit card in the computer that connects the computer to a network. See "Bus Topology" in Chapter 4 and "Network Workstations" in Chapter 1.

network operating system The operating systems that is usually ran on file servers. This operating system provides the capabilites to share files and devices across a network. See "A Basic Network" in Chapter 1.

network pipes A networking protocol that allows information to be shared between network processes. See "Network Pipe" in Chapter 6.

network repeater A device that receives a data packet from one network and rebroadcasts the packet onto another network. No routing information is added to the protocol. See "Repeaters" in Chapter 8.

NFS See *network file system.*

NIC See *network interface card.*

NOS See *network operating system.*

open system interconnection reference model. An international standard for LAN architecture, established by ISO and IEEE. The OSI model is important primarily because it attempts to establish hardware independence. See "Introduction to the OSI Model" in Chapter 3.

operating system The software that runs on a computer that provides user access to local computer hardware.

OSI model See *Open System Interconnection reference model.*

packet A collection of data and control information to be sent over a network. See "Token-Based Networks" in Chapter 6 and "OSI Media Layers" in Chapter 3.

parallel port A port that supports the synchronous, high-speed flow of data along parallel lines. This is the type of port usually used for printers.

passive An electronic device that does not condition an electrical or electroic signal. See "Network Interconnection" in Chapter 5.

patch cable A wire used to interconnect devices. See "Wiring with Efficiency" in Chapter 4.

patch panel A collection of connectors which can be interconnected with patch cables. See "Wiring with Efficiency" in Chapter 4.

peer-to-peer A networking architecture that treats all network stations as equal partners. See "Peer-To-Peer LANs" in Chapter 7.

peripheral device A device—such as a printer, disk drive, or tape drive—connected to and controlled by a computer, that is external to the computer's CPU. See "Sharing on a Network" in Chapter 1.

physical address The hardware address of a network device. See "Routers" in Chapter 8.

point-to-point See "Point-to-Point Communication" in Chapter 9.

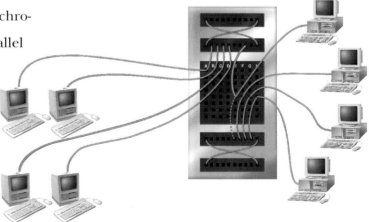

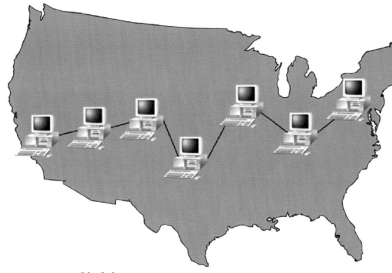

polishing
The process of removing blemishes and scratches from a fiber-optic cable prior to attaching a connector. See "Fiber-Optic Cable and Connectors" in Chapter 5.

preamble A sequence of bits at the beginning of a token packet. See "Token-Based Networks" in Chapter 6.

Presentation Layer The OSI model layer responsible for data encryption and compression. See "OSI Host Layers" and "Introduction to the OSI Model" in Chapter 3.

print server A network device that allows printers to be connected and shared with other network resources. See "Print Servers" in Chapter 8.

protocol converter A device used to change the format of a network packet. See "Gateways" in Chapter 8.

PVC Polyvinyl chloride. A plastic used to cover wires and cables. See "Fiber-Optic Cable and Connectors" in Chapter 5.

quad The telephone cable used most. Colored red, green, yellow, and black. See "Unshielded Twisted Pair Cable" in Chapter 5.

read access Privileges allowing an object to examine information, and even to copy it, but not to modify or delete it. See "Peer-To-Peer LANs" in Chapter 7.

real-time An event that must be responded to immediately. See "Wiring with Efficiency" in Chapter 4.

registered jack A modular connector used in telephone and computer networks for unshielded twisted pair cable. See also RJ-11 and RJ-45. See "Unshielded Twisted Pair Cable" in Chapter 5.

RPC Remote procedure call. A programming interface that allows remote computers to access information stored on a host or remote system See "SPX/IPX" in Chapter 6.

resistor An electrical device used to control the flow of electrons. See "Coaxial Cable Connectors" in Chapter 5.

ring A term used in the telephone industry. The term comes from the days of a switchboard when all connections went to a connector. The ring is the back part of the connector. See "Unshielded Twisted Pair Cable" in Chapter 5.

RIP Routing Information Protocol. A protocol that helps route a network message between nodes. See "SPX/IPX" in Chapter 6.

RJ-11 A six-wire connector used for telephones. See "Unshielded Twisted Pair Cable" in Chapter 5.

RJ-45 An eight-wire connector used for telephones and computer networks. See "Unshielded Twisted Pair Cable" in Chapter 5.

router A device that moves information between networks at the logical address level. See "Routers" in Chapter 8.

save sets See *backup library.*

serial transmission Sending data by individual bits. See "Terminal Connections and Mainframes" in Chapter 1.

serial port A port that information is sent out in individual bits. An RS232C port is an example of this type of port.

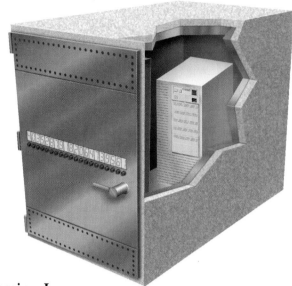

Session Layer

The layer of the OSI model responsible for error correction and dialogue control. See "Introduction to the OSI Model" in Chapter 3.

shield The foil or webbed covering of a coaxial cable. See "Coaxial Cable" in Chapter 5.

signal Electrical information. See "Coaxial Cable" in Chapter 5.

silver satin (slang) Flat cable, usually silver in color, used to connect telephones and network devices to wall jacks. See "Unshielded Twisted Pair Cable" in Chapter 5.

single-user A computer that allows only one person at a time to use it. See "Comparison of Single-User Operating Systems and NOS" in Chapter 7.

SNMP Simple Network Management Protocol. See "Print Servers" in Chapter 8.

software license An agreement on the usage of a software product. See "Sharing on a Network" in Chapter 1.

source-routing bridge A network device that must be programmed with all network addresses at installation time. When network nodes are added or dropped, the bridge must be reprogrammed. Compare to *transparent bridge*. See "Bridges" in Chapter 8.

spanning-tree algorithm A computer algorithm used in bridges that helps to determine the location of new network nodes and the shortest path between network devices. See "Bridges" in Chapter 8.

ST connector A special connector used on fiber-optic cable. See "Fiber-Optic Cable and Connectors" in Chapter 5.

star network A physical network topology that has a center point, where a network hub is placed. Individual cable runs extend from the center hub to each workstation. See "Star Topology" in Chapter 4.

start bits A signal at the beginning of a sequence of bits used to tell the receiving device to get ready to receive data. See "Asynchronous Communication" in Chapter 9.

SOH Start Of Header. See "ARCnet Network" in Chapter 6.

stop bits A signal used to indicate the end of a data transmission. See "Asynchronous Communication" in Chapter 9.

system scheduler A special program that runs in a computer operating system to determine when other programs can run, to negotiate the best times for disk accesses to occur, and to time the resources of the operating system. See "How A Network Operating System Works" in Chapter 7.

T-Connector A BNC connector that allows three devices or cables to be interconnected. See "Coaxial Cable Connectors" in Chapter 5.

T1 A communication line available from a local telecommunication provider. This line contains 28 56-kbps channels. See "T1 and T3" in Chapter 9.

T3 28 T1 lines. See "T1 and T3" in Chapter 9.

TDM See *time division multiplexor*.

Teflon A fireproof material used to insulate cables and wires. See "Coaxial Cable" in Chapter 5.

teleconferencing Interactive communication between meeting participants at different locations. See "Video Conferencing" in Chapter 1.

terminal server See "Saving Through Device Sharing" in Chapter 2.

termination Process of connecting the ends of a cable to a connector or wall plate. See "Bus Topology" in Chapter 4.

terminator An electrical device that usually contains a resistor; used to tune a network cable. See "Coaxial Cable Connectors" in Chapter 5.

time division multiplexor A multiplexor that divides network bandwidth into individual time slots. See "Time Division Multiplexing" in Chapter 9.

tip The end of a phone cable. See "Unshielded Twisted Pair" in Chapter 5.

token A special symbol that enables a network device to access the network. See "Token-Based Networks" in Chapter 6.

topology Used to describe a type of network architecture and particularly to describe the wiring methods used in implementing a network. Some of the common network topologies are bus and star. See "Bus Topology" and "Star Topology' in Chapter 4.

transceiver A modem that can transmit and receive signals, which may include computer data via radio frequencies. See "Wireless LANs" in Chapter 4.

transparent bridge A network device that learns network addresses once in operation. Compare to *source-routing bridge*. See "Bridges" in Chapter 8.

Transport Layer The layer of the OSI model responsible for reliable data delivery. See "Introduction to the OSI Model" in Chapter 3.

user interface A special program that is designed to graphically interact with both the computer user and the computer. See "OSI Host Layers" in Chapter 3.

user pack license A software license that allows a given number of concurrent accesses to a program. See "Software Licensing" in Chapter 2.

user name A string of characters used to identify a computer user. See "File Server Login" in Chapter 2.

virtual network In a LAN environment, the network that is formed between a workstation and transceivers. See "Wireless LANs" in Chapter 4.

virus shield A special memory-resident program that constantly monitors and watches a computer system for viruses. See "Virus Protection" in Chapter 2.

wire A conductor used to carry electricity or information. See "Sharing on a Network" in Chapter 1.

wireless A network topology that uses radio waves for communication between workstations and file servers. See "Wireless LANs" in Chapter 4.

workgroup computing Sharing information and resources between members of a project team or department. See "Workgroup Computing" in Chapter 2.

workgroup software The computing model that is used to describe the sharing of *information*, e-mail, and resources through a computer network.

workstation A personal computer or any station at which users interact and use computer resources. See "Star Topology" in Chapter 4.

write access Permission given to an object to modify information in a particular file or directory. See "Peer-To-Peer LANs" in Chapter 7.

X.25 A recommendation for a public network service that has been adopted and widely used for most wide-area networks. See "X.25" in Chapter 9.

INDEX

SYMBOLS

10BASET, 194

A

access control databases, 194
accessing files, 39-40
accounting, *see* network
    accounting
ACK (handshaking), 194
air plenum, 194
alert fields, 194
analog signals, 24
antennas, 194
Application Layer (OSI model),
    62, 194
application sharing, 37-38
applications, 194
        control files, 54
        see also programs; software
archive collections, 184
ARCnet communication
    protocols, 102-103
ASCII (American Standard Code
    for Information Interchange),
    22-23, 194
ASK (amplitude shift keying),
    161, 194
asynchronous communications,
    158-159, 194
asynchronous servers, 32, 195
ATT258A standard, 89
AUI (attachment user interface),
    195
authentication process, 33-34, 195

B

backbone (networks), 70-71, 195
backup devices, 195
backup libraries, 184-185, 195
backup procedures (files), 182-183
        file server-based, 188-189
        network backup stations,
            190-191
        remote workstations, 192-193
        tape rotation, 186-187
backup stations, 195
baseband LAN communications,
    24-26
binary, 195
bit packing, 178-179
block licenses (software), 53-54
BNC (Bayone-Neill-Concelman)
    connectors, 84-85, 93, 195
boot PROM, 94, 195
bps (bits per second), 19
bridges, 134-135, 138-139, 196
broadband LAN communications,
    27
brouters, 138, 196
bus topology, 70-71, 196

C

cable pairs, 196
cabling, 196
        cable management, 76
        BNC (Bayone-Neill-
            Concelman) connectors,
            84-85
        coaxial, 82-85
        connectors, 84-85
        fiber optic, 90-91
        network interconnection,
            96-97
        NIC, 94-95
        pairs, 198
        star topology, 72
        troubleshooting, 92-93
        unshielded twisted pair, 86-89
cache (memory), 131, 196
campus networks, 10-11
carrier waves, 26
carriers, 196
Category 3 (UTP), 196

Category 4 (UTP), 196
Category 5 (UTP), 196
CATV, 196
CCITT, 196
CDDI (Copper Distributed Data
    Interface), 106, 198
central office, 196
central processing unit, *see* CPU
character sets (ASCII), 22-23
checksum, 196
cladding (cables), 90, 197
cleaning software (viruses), 49
client/server model, 197
coaxial cable, 82-85, 197
command interpreter, 197
communication protocols, 197
        ARCnet, 102-103
        EtherNet, 108-109
        FDDI, 106-107
        IPX, 110-111
        pipes, 114-115
        SPX, 110-111
        TCP/IP, 112-113
        Token Ring, 104-105
        token-passing networks,
            100-101
communications, 32
        asynchronous, 158-159
        baseband LANs, 25-26
        broadband LANs, 27
        data compressing, 178-79
        data encryption, 176-177
        data transfer rates, 19-20
        frame relay networks, 174-175
        frequency division multi-
            plexing, 168-169
        modems, 162-163
        modulation, 160-161
        multiplexors, 153, 164-165
        point-to-point, 154-155
        synchronous, 156-157
        T1/T3 links, 170-171
        time division multiplexing,
            166-167
        X.25 protocol, 172-173
compressing data, 178-179
computer buses, 17, 197
concentrators, 72, 96, 197
conductors, 198
connection-oriented
    communications, 198
connectionless communications,
    198

connectors, 198
    cabling, 84-85
    RJ-45, 89
    ST-type, 90
continuous signals, 24
control characters, 198
control files (applications), 54
core, 198
CPU (central processing unit),
    16, 196
CRC (cyclic redundancy check), 198

D

data compression, 178-179, 198
data encryption, 176-177, 199
data fields (FDDI), 107
Data Link Layer (OSI model), 67
data switches, 199
data transfer rates, 19-20
demodulators, 199
demultiplexors, 165
DES (data encryption standard),
    177
destination mux, 166-167
device drivers, 121, 199
digital signals, 24
direct memory access, *see* DMA
directory services (NOS), 126-127
DMA (direct memory access),
    17, 199
documents, sharing, 41-42
DOS, *see* NOS
dumb terminals, 21, 147
duty cycle, 199

E

E-mail, 199
EBCDIC (Extended Binary-Coded
    Decimal Interchange Code),
    22, 199
electrical isolation, 90, 199
encrypting data, 176-177, 199
EOT (end of transmission), 199
error checking, 199
error correction, 199

EtherNet
    communication protocols,
      108-109
    cabling, 88, 92
exclusive write access, 40
extended LANs, 200

F

falling edges, 200
FAX modems, 32
FBE (Free Buffer Enquiry), 102
FDDI (Fiber Distributed Data
    Interface), 106-107, 200
fiber-optic cables, 90-91, 200
file servers, 8, 131, 200
    backups, 188-189
    login process, 33-34
    logout process, 35-36
    security issues, 47-48
files
    accessing, 39-40
    backup libraries, 184-187
    backups, 182-183
    concurrent access, 42
    encryption, 176-177
    exclusive write access, 40
    locking, 39
    read-only access, 40
    read-write access, 40
    virus protection, 49-50
filters, 200
flow control, 200
frame controls (FDDI), 107
frame relay networks, 174-175, 200
frames, 200
frequency division multiplexing,
    168-169, 200
FSK (frequency shift keying), 161

G-H

gateways
grandfather method (tape back-
    ups), 186-187, 201
ground potential, 201

hard drives, 183-185
host address field, 201
Host Layers (OSI model), 62-64
hubs, 72, 96-97, 201

I-K

IEEE (Institute of Electrical and
    Electronic Engineers), 60
    IEEE 802.3 (Ethernet)
      standard, 201
    IEEE 802.5 (Token Ring)
      standard, 201
impedance, 201
iNDX, 118
input/output ports, 201
interference, 201
international networks, 15
internetworks, 201
interrupts, 129, 201
IP addresses, 136, 202
IPX (Internetwork Packet
    Exchange)
    communication protocols,
      110-111
    print servers, 147
ISO (International Standards
    Organization), 60, 202
ITT (Invitation to Transmit),
    102, 202

kernel, 202
kevlar, 202

L

LANs (local area networks), 8
    baseboard LANs, 24-26
    broadband LANs, 27
    peer-to-peer, 128-129
    repeaters, 141
    server-based, 130-131
    teleconferencing, 29
    wireless, 78-79
layering (networks), 60-61
    Host Layers, 62-64
    Media Layers, 66-67